Coffee and Coffeehouses

COFFEE AND COFFEEHOUSES

The Origins of a Social Beverage in the Medieval Near East

RALPH S. HATTOX

UNIVERSITY OF WASHINGTON PRESS
Seattle and London

Cover illustration: Turkish miniature *(detail)*: mid-sixteenth century.
(Courtesy of the Trustees of the Chester Beatty Library)

Coffee and Coffeehouses was originally published in 1985 as No. 3 in Near Eastern Studies, University of Washington, sponsored by the Department of Near Eastern Languages and Civilization and the Middle East Center of the Henry M. Jackson School of International Studies, University of Washington.

University of Washington Press edition, 1988
Third printing, 1996
Printed in the United States of America

Library of Congress Cataloging-in-Publication Data
Hattox, Ralph S.
Coffee and coffeehouses.
Reprint. Originally published: Seattle: Distributed by University of Washington Press, c1985. Originally published in series: Near Eastern studies, University of Washington: no. 3
Bibliography: p.
Includes index
1. Coffee—Middle East—History. 2. Coffee-houses—Middle East—History. 3. Coffee—History. 4. Coffee-houses—History.
I. Title.
GT2919.M628H38 1988 394.1'2 87–31618
ISBN 0–295–96231–3

The paper used in this publication meets the minimum requirements of American National Standard for Information Sciences—Permanence of Paper for Printed Library Materials, ANSI Z39.48–1984. ∞

To my parents

CONTENTS

ILLUSTRATIONS

Following page 52

PREFACE

I began writing this book some seven years ago as a short seminar paper at Princeton. Faced with the task of investigating the application of Islamic law to some specific question, I chose that of the prohibition of coffee. Starting with the knowledge that coffee was eventually found licit by the major schools of law, what remained was to examine the process of legal reasoning through which coffee was originally condemned, and how this condemnation was ultimately overturned. Several months of research led to the perplexing realization that coffee was eventually found licit because the original prohibition was not just faulty, but based on such flimsy claims that one had to wonder why they were put forward to begin with. If coffee itself patently fell within the group of legal beverages, there must be something with which it was associated that prompted all the furor. This work is an effort to discover what that something was.

A few methodological problems had to be tackled in dealing with the question. To begin with, while a fair amount of contemporary material exists concerning the coffee debate of the sixteenth century, which indeed forms the core of the work, much valuable material from a later age was found, and many of these works furnished detail that could be found in no other place. In light of this, I chose to depart in places from the sound principle of not judging the activities of a society by the writings about it from a later age. Lane's *Manners and Customs*, for example, suffers the dual disability of being of a much later time and of looking at the everyday life of Muḥammad ʿAlī's Egypt from an unabashedly European point of view. Nonetheless the detail Lane furnishes concerning the operation of coffeehouses in Cairo in his own day is simply too valuable to be overlooked. In those places where I do employ such later writers, I try to make it clear that we cannot necessarily interpret events of the sixteenth century by nineteenth-century evidence, and that such evidence must only be taken with this warning always in mind.

The focus of the work as well has some bearing on methodology. While archival materials have become the mainstay of studies concerned with the activities of states or officials, or with economic life, they are far more burdensome than fruitful to a work such as this, with its emphasis on mentalities, on the attitude of an entire society to the introduction of something entirely new to its fabric. The activities of the governments involved, and especially the economic impact of coffee in the Near East, deserve books of their own, and lie quite outside the scope of the present work.

I feel it necessary here to say a word or two about the system of transliteration I employ. For Turkish words, wherever possible, I prefer to use modern Turkish orthography, although at times I include extra diacritical marks to indicate the original spelling. For Arabic, I have tried to stick throughout to a somewhat modified version of the Library of Congress system of transliteration. I depart from this system in that, with nouns ending with a *tā' marbūṭa* that are not in construct with a following noun, I have chosen not to employ a potentially confusing (and to my mind ugly) final *h*. In addition, while I follow convention in dropping almost all inflectional endings from nouns, I have retained those denoting the indefinite accusative, particularly where this case is used adverbially. This ending I have retained in the form of a superscript *an*, for instance, *majāz*^{an}.

In the years since I began this work I have benefited greatly from the assistance of numerous institutions and individuals. First of all, I should like to acknowledge the help provided by the staffs of the following libraries, who provided me with microfilms and photocopies of manuscripts, and photographs of some of the illustrations used in this work: the Division of Rare Books, Library of Congress; the National Library of Medicine in Bethesda, Maryland, the Bibliothèque nationale, Paris; the Escurial, Madrid; the Staatsbibliothek Preußischer Kulturbesitz, Berlin; the library of the Rijksuniversitet, Leiden; the Chester Beatty Library, Dublin; New York Public Library; and Princeton University Library. Special thanks go as well to Paul E. Chevedden, UCLA; Martha Dukas, Boston Public Library; Edward W. Earle, California Museum of Photography; George S. Hobart, Library of Congress; Mary Ellen Taylor, Harvard Semitic Museum; and Kristin Kinsey, Suzzallo Library, University of Washington.

I should also like to express my gratitude to the many teachers, colleagues, and friends who offered bibliographical suggestions and valuable comments on the numerous draft versions of this work, particularly Avrom Udovitch, Charles Issawi, Norman Itzkowitz, Bernard Lewis, the late Rudolf Mach, Halil İnalcık, Lawrence Conrad, Paula

Sanders, and Shaun Marmon. Thanks also go to Grace Edelman of the Department of Near Eastern Studies at Princeton for her support during much of the writing of the dissertation on which this book is based.

Finally, I wish to acknowledge a special debt to three people who were of tremendous assistance during the final stages of the preparation of this work: Daniel Goffman, for his copious comments and criticisms of the original manuscript; John R. Coogan, whose critical eye has, I hope, kept my prose from drifting too far toward the purple; and above all, Felicia J. Hecker of the University of Washington Press for the care, attention, and seemingly boundless energy she has put into preparing this work for publication.

COFFEE AND COFFEEHOUSES

CHAPTER 1

The Great Coffee Controversy

Coffee has never been a mere beverage. Some three centuries have passed since it became the overnight rage among the fashionable and witty in cities throughout Europe. Even in the late twentieth century, however, it has yet to be relegated to the ranks of the more pedestrian potions with which we quench our thirst or warm our insides. Little of coffee's original mystique has been worn off by centuries of familiarity.

What is true for contemporary Western society was all the more so for that of the sixteenth-century Near East in the decades following coffee's sudden emergence from the obscure corners of the Yemen. Among other things, it was a commodity for speculation, a symbol of hospitality, an excuse for sociable procrastination. It also became one of the great legal, intellectual, and literary obsessions of the age, around which an intense, if sporadic, debate raged in the capitals and metropolises of Islam from Adrianople to Aden. Echoes of the innumerable speeches, harangues, and imprecations that were pronounced on the subject reach us in chronicles, legal opinions, and governmental edicts, and in the handful of extant contemporary treatises written specifically on the virtues, salubrity, and legality of coffee. Coffee became a question that received attention in the highest circles. Successive potentates took mutually contradictory stands on coffee, and governmental policy concerning the drink tended to be as mutable as the composition of the sovereign's inner circle. In the semiofficial class of legal scholars and judges, a gaping rift appeared between the fanatical opponents of the drink and its sometimes equally fanatical supporters. Dozens saw fit to set down their thoughts on the topic; many such writers are known to posterity for little else, while occasionally literary lights of considerably more brilliance, such as the renowned seventeenth-century Ottoman author and bibliographer Kâtib Çelebi, had among their minor efforts works on coffee. In many places blood as well as words flowed—there were persecutions in Istanbul, pro- and anti-coffee riots in Cairo, and recurring raids on coffeehouses and seizures of property made in the name of public morality, sometimes by the highest circles of government, but more often at the initiative of minor officials, generally for reasons known best to themselves.

All this, of course, is bright, colorful stuff, the kind of thing about which some European, searching for an acceptably exotic subject, might have written a light opera in the fashion of Mozart's *Die Entführung aus dem Serail*. Regrettably, these incidents have often provided ammunition for those whose love for ridicule far exceeds their capacity for understanding a society other than their own. Stories of this sort have appeared in the sections on beverages in innumerable cookbooks, the authors often adding their own embarrassingly offensive explanations for this seemingly petty and irrational behavior over a trifling matter.

Fortunately, the great coffee controversy has also been the subject of the occasional learned monograph. Some, such as E. Birnbaum ("Vice Triumphant," *Durham University Journal* [Dec. 1956]: 21–27), have presented the outlines of the various incidents in a manner both engaging and scholarly. Others have striven for greater condensation and concision—most notable of these latter was C. van Arendonk, who packed into four pages of *The Encyclopaedia of Islam* (reprinted in the second edition) a detailed distillation of the use of coffee in Islamic society, culled from an impressive collection of primary and secondary sources. Yet while these and dozens of other scholars of the past four centuries, from the Italian botanist, Prospero Alpini (Alpinus; 1553–1617) on down, have contributed much to the understanding of the problem, they all miss (or, perhaps more accurately, choose not to elaborate on) what I believe to be the central point in the whole affair—what is, indeed, the point of departure of the present work.

This, is that in spite of what is sometimes perceived by Western tastes as fruitless quibbling over a concern of very little importance, an example of the petty-mindedness of a hidebound religious institution carried to its illogical extreme, these people most certainly were deadly serious about the subject. If we dismiss the opposition to coffee (as did not only later Western writers, but even their own contemporaries and coreligionists) as Muslim bluenoses, fired by their own pervertedly rigid concept of Islamic law and proper behavior, haughtily and righteously preaching against even the most innocent of earthly pleasures, we not only do them a disservice, but ourselves as well, for in adopting such a stance we become mere participants in a debate that has been dead and cold for three hundred years. If, however, we assume there to be some slightly more rational explanation for the opposition to the use of coffee and the patronage of public coffeehouses, we can possibly win insights into the way in which the urban intellectual of the sixteenth century saw his society, and why some saw a threat to that society through the use of coffee.

This in fact is what is so useful about the records of such debates: it is not that they furnish us with colorful anecdotes (though indeed they supply these in abundance), but rather that they reflect the serious concerns of generally sober and reasonable men.

In studying the body of available literature, either by contemporary writers or later scholars, on the controversy over coffee, one inevitably runs up against a handful of traditional explanations for the rise and growth of opposition to coffee drinking. In most cases these consist of one or more of the following:

1. Coffee was thought in some way physically or chemically so constituted as to make its consumption a violation of Islamic law, either because it was intoxicating or physically harmful, or because some step in its preparation, such as roasting the beans beyond the point of carbonization, made it unacceptable.
2. Coffee was rejected by the ultrapious simply because it was an innovation, *bid'a*.
3. The political activities that became an important part of the social life of the coffeehouse grew increasingly alarming to the governmental elite.
4. The patrons of the coffeehouse indulged in a variety of improper pastimes, ranging from gambling to involvement in irregular and criminally unorthodox sexual situations, and as such attracted the attention of those officials who were assigned the custodianship of public morality.

In referring to these explanations as traditional, in no way do I wish to convey any sense of pejorative comparison. Quite the contrary: each of them, and particularly the last two, is a relatively faithful distillation of the arguments raised against coffee. Individually or collectively, they are, as far as they go, generally valid explanations of anti-coffee prohibitionary sentiment. Much of what will be said in the coming chapters will be a reaffirmation of the theories and interpretations of previous writers, reinforcing them with new evidence.

Nonetheless, these explanations seem in another sense curiously inadequate and hollow. When one studies the circumstances surrounding the cases where for one of the aforementioned reasons coffee is prohibited, coffeehouses are closed down, or both, one often detects a curious pattern of events. In essence, what seems to happen is that the prohibitionist, on learning of the drink or the establishment, is first filled with a vague sense of uneasiness about it; it is only then that he sets about to collect the evidence that eventually leads to an official proclamation, a legal opinion, or a mere moral harangue against it. There are other reasons, not explicitly enumerated or detailed, which contribute to the protagonist's initial alarm and subsequent interest in coffee. We may actually consider these other reasons to be the prime movers toward prohibitionist feelings, more important than the explicitly enunciated arguments by which, through long investigation and perhaps a bit of creative fiddling, the already resolute opponent of coffee furnishes himself with legal artillery. In addition, one often finds vaguely sketched objections to things that cannot be pinned down and condemned as contrary to the precepts of the holy law, but which are nevertheless irksome, censurable, and generally objectionable in the context of uncodified cultural tradition.

In order to exploit fully the accounts of a controversy such as that over coffee, one must look at it as more than a series of confrontations between the advocates of various positions, as more than an interesting and intriguing case study of the applications of Islamic law and legal reasoning. The problem is one of pushing the questions one step beyond those that have already been asked. One may very well ask, What are the reasons and explanations generally given in our sources for the pious and official opposition to coffee? or What are the arguments used and the systems of reasoning applied? The answers to such questions furnish one with a good start, but only that. A further level of understanding requires that a different sort of question be asked: Why would such objections arise in the first place? What sort of alarming signals did those who began to question the legality of the practice sense as being emitted from the use of coffee or from the patronage of the coffeehouse? and finally, Were these signals indeed indicative of a social or moral change—of which the coffeehouse was a symptom, a catalyst, or both—that produced a shift in the relations among men and gave rise to new habits and attitudes reaching beyond the café? It is in this that the scope of the present work lies.

The extent to which we can hope to answer these questions is of necessity governed by the type and quality of source material available, and here we find ourselves opening a rather mixed bag. On the negative side, we become instantly aware that what seems important to us, what we wish to study in minute detail, is in reality but a rather insignificant incident in the history of things as a whole, at least history as contemporary chroniclers perceived it. The introduction of coffee and the debate over it were not events of monumental or immediately perceptible significance, except to those involved. No states rose or fell as a consequence of the introduction of coffee, no cities were put under siege, no populations put to the sword, nobody of any great importance ever lost his head in the largely verbal confrontation. Great fortunes were indeed amassed in the coffee trade, and a few cities and regions experienced measurable, if temporary, economic revitalization owing to a position on coffee trade routes. These were developments, however, of the years after the debate had died down. Coffee, the coffeehouse, and the accompanying practices that had been perceived as threats early on, had by that time been embraced by and thoroughly integrated into the society. They had become venerable and revered parts of public and private life, no longer to be regarded as dangerous innovations. What we are left with for the earliest period, then, are historical table-scraps, a page here, a sentence there, from which we must piece together much of our discussion and chronology.

If the chronicles fail us, however, there are three rather more useful types of sources: legal writings, contemporary treatises written specifically about coffee, and travelers' accounts. Legal sources—handbooks on practical jurisprudence, collections of *fatwās* (legal opinions) and the like—may first be thought of as having great promise, but will often fail to deliver the goods. Ottoman *fatwās* can be particularly disappointing. One will often encounter a carefully phrased question that deals with just the subject at hand. Hoping for several pages of discussion, drawing from Qur'ān, prophetic precedent, and subtle analogy in the best classical style, the reader suddenly finds that the mufti has simply left him hanging with a terse *olur* (it is permitted) or *olmaz* (it is not permitted). True, one does have the answer to the question, but very little concerning the process of arriving at that answer.

Far more useful are the treatises on coffee itself, which are discussed at length in the Appendix. Only a few general points need be made here. First, we are primarily speaking of those treatises written by Muslim scholars. There were many written by Europeans, but these must be considered along with the travelers' accounts, since they are more or less elaborations on one of the curiosities of the Orient.

One must always bear in mind that the treatises written by Muslim scholars are almost exclusively polemical. The authors wrote not to present an objective and balanced discussion of the subject, but to present the point of whatever faction they belonged to. As long as we approach these works with more than even the usual caution, they can be particularly valuable.

Finally, a word about travelers' accounts. Perhaps because it was the essence of their function that they record and relate the bizarre, the new, and those things unlike anything that they observed in their native lands, European travelers of the late sixteenth and early seventeenth centuries offer quite a bit concerning what they first appreciated as a singularly repellent beverage. Admittedly, some accounts fall rather flat. Augier Ghislain de Busbecq (1522–92), Emperor Ferdinand I's ambassador to the court of Sultan Süleyman I, for instance, was in Istanbul at about the time when the first cafés appeared there, a time when the sultan had even appointed a *kahvecibaşı* (chief coffee-cook) at the palace. Nonetheless, Busbecq thought it to the advantage of his diplomatic mission to remain in his apartment for almost the entire duration of his stay, and, in consequence, observed very little of the everyday life of the city. Busbecq was undoubtedly a diplomat of considerable skill, but one cannot help but get the impression that he was a bit of a prig as well.

Fortunately, there were other travelers with a more highly developed sense of curiosity. Among the most notable of these were the English poet, Sir George Sandys (1577–1644), the French traveler, Jean de Thévenot (1633–67) and, though of a later period, the German traveler and explorer, Carsten Niebuhr (1733–1815). Niebuhr is particularly valuable because of the look he gives us of the areas of the Yemen where coffee cultivation first developed, while Sandys and Thévenot were men of uncommonly keen powers of observation. At their best European travelers could supply accurate detail concerning the everyday life they saw around them, but one must always beware of their tendency to pass on unverified rumor simply because it made a good tale for their readers.

CHAPTER 2

The Coming of Coffee to the Near East

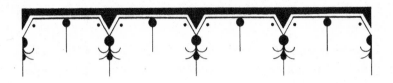

Coffee came into general use in the lands of Islam sometime in the mid-fifteenth century. Owing to the virtual silence with which the beverage insinuated itself into the society, it is impossible to attribute a more specific date to its arrival. The problem is in part one arising from the nature of historical writing in the premodern Middle East. The chronicle and biography were the archetypes for dealing with and writing about the past, and these necessarily are concerned with what might be called landmark events—deaths of notable persons, uprisings, coups d'état, plagues, and invasions. Since the introduction of items of material culture, such as comestibles, can only be called an invasion in the most figurative sense of the word, there is not the immediate awareness and recording that inevitably attends the arrival of a real army. The tendency of real armies to be noticed makes the job of the political historian, at least in establishing a relatively accurate chronology, a bit easier. Such a historian of a few centuries later must reconcile the dates given in his sources with other information, and with his own powers of reason, but generally he is working within a fairly narrow stretch of time. On the other hand, an item of material culture—a tool, an invention, a new foodstuff, or something similar—generally slips into an area unnoticed, or at least unrecorded by the contemporary annalist. It may be only sometime later that mention, either direct or indirect, is made of the item's presence in an area. The best the historian working a few centuries later can hope to do is establish a *terminus ad quem* for the introduction of the subject under discussion and proceed into areas for which something more certain can be said.

Actually, with coffee we are not faced with quite so dismal a situation. For reasons that will become apparent in subsequent chapters, the coming of coffee was noticed and recorded within a comparatively short time. The fact is that as soon as it became widespread, coffee did indeed draw the attention of those who wrote letters, essays, legal decisions, and books, to the extent that the reputation of coffee often preceded its actual arrival in an area. Coffee had, in brief, become something of a hot topic. Once this happened, the question began to be asked, When did this first appear? and it seems that there were still many around who could remember when it was not known, or who at least remembered their first encounter with it as something extraordinary. Thus, one is able to speak in round terms of decades, while some historians who deal with such vitally important items as the stirrup are forced into vague debates where centuries hang in the balance.

THE ORIGINS OF THE USE OF COFFEE

Later Arab writers of chronicles were quite aware of a gap existing in their knowledge of the origins of coffee, and some could not resist the temptation to include pious legends to supplement their material. Abū al-Ṭayyib al-Ghazzī (brother of the biographer Najm al-Dīn [1570–1651, A.H. 977–1061]) relates an account in which Solomon appears as the first to make use of coffee.[1] According to

Abū al-Ṭayyib, Solomon was said to have come in his travels to a town whose inhabitants were afflicted with some unspecified disease. On the command of the angel Gabriel, he roasted coffee beans "from the Yemen," from which he brewed the drink, which when given to the sufferers, cured them of their illness. The report concludes by saying that coffee was then completely forgotten until the beginning of the tenth [A.D. sixteenth] century.[2]

Most writers, however, were content to limit their histories to the more recent past. Coffee, or at least the consumption of the fruit of the coffee plant—a distinction that will be discussed later—is usually traced to Ethiopia. It is there that those who are traditionally credited with introducing it into general use in the Islamic world are said to have first seen it.[3] European writers of the seventeenth century commonly embellish the story with accounts of how it first came into use there, such as the tale of the shepherd who noticed the uncommon vigor of his sheep after they had just grazed on the plant.[4] It is far from clear where they got such tales. Whatever the case may be, the Arabs who wrote on coffee would have none of this sort of legend, be it of Arab or Western inspiration. The most important of sixteenth-century writers on coffee ʿAbd al-Qādir al-Jazīrī (fl. 1558), after speaking of the introduction of coffee to the Yemen, cautions the reader:

> We say [that this account pertains to] the Yemen alone [lit., not anywhere else] because the appearance of coffee [was] in the land of Ibn Saʿd al-Dīn and the country of the Abyssinians and of the Jabart, and other places of the land of the ʿAjam, but the time of its first [use] is unknown, nor do we know the reason.[5]

In any event, such considerations are not of great importance to the early Arab writers, since their main interest is to establish when and where it came to the Arab-Muslim lands, and, of equal importance, by whom and for what reasons it was introduced.

Throughout the various stories and legends that have come down to us concerning the origins of coffee drinking in the central Islamic lands, there is general agreement on two points. First, the use of coffee is almost invariably traced to the Yemen.[6] Second, most stories connect it to a man or men of one of the mystical Sufi religious orders, to which coffee quickly became important for devotional purposes. It is from this point that the stories diverge. An examination of each of them in turn sheds light not only on the question with which we are immediately concerned, but also on early attitudes, symbols, and concepts associated with coffee.

The first account that is given by Jazīrī is related on the authority of Shihāb al-Dīn ibn 'Abd al-Ghaffār, an early writer on coffee whose work provided Jazīrī with much of his material.

At the beginning of this [the sixteenth] century, the news reached us in Egypt that a drink, called *qahwa*, had spread in the Yemen and was being used by Sufi shaykhs and others to help them stay awake during their devotional exercises, which they perform according to their well-known Way (*'alā ṭarīqatihim al-mashhūra*). Then it reached us, some time later, that its appearance and spread there had been due to the efforts of the learned shaykh, imam, mufti, and Sufi Jamāl al-Dīn Abū 'Abd Allāh Muḥammad ibn Sa'īd, known as al-Dhabḥānī.... We heard that he had been in charge of the critical review of *fatwā*s in Aden, which at that time was a job whose holder decided whether *fatwā*s were sound or in need of revision, which he would indicate at the bottom of the document in his own hand. The reason for his introducing coffee, according to what we heard, was that some affair had forced him to leave Aden and go to Ethiopia, where he stayed for some time. [There] he found the people using *qahwa*, though he knew nothing of its characteristics. After he had returned to Aden, he fell ill, and remembering [*qahwa*], he drank it and benefited by it. He found that among its properties was that it drove away fatigue and lethargy, and brought to the body a certain sprightliness and vigor. In consequence, when he became a Sufi, he and other Sufis in Aden began to use the beverage made from it, as we have said. Then the whole people—both the learned and the common—followed [his example] in drinking it, seeking help in study and other vocations and crafts, so that it continued to spread.

[When we heard all this,] I wrote to one of our brothers in God, one of the people of learning and religion in Zabīd [a town in the Yemen], the jurist Jamāl al-Dīn Abū 'Abd Allāh Muḥammad ibn 'Abd al-Ghaffār Bā-'Alawī[7] ... asking that he inform me of which of the people of learning and faith, people whose opinions are respected, drank it, and of its first appearance.... He answered: "I asked a group of elders in our country [about the appearance of coffee], the oldest of whom at present is my uncle, the jurist Wajīh al-Dīn 'Abd al-Raḥmān ibn Ibrāhīm al-'Alawī—a man over ninety—and he told me ... 'I was at the town of Aden, and there came to us some poor Sufi, who was making and drinking coffee, and who made it as well for the learned jurist Muḥammad Bā-Faḍl al-Ḥaḍramī,[8] the highest jurist at the port of Aden, and for ... Muḥammad al-Dhabḥānī. These two drank it with a company of people, for whom their example was sufficient.'"

It is possible that al-Dhabḥānī was the first to introduce [coffee] to Aden, as he is reputed [to have done], or it is possible that someone else introduced it, but it is associated with him because it was he who was responsible for its emergence and spread. Al-Dhabḥānī died in the year 875 [A.D. 1470–71].[9]

This account provides very valuable clues concerning the advent of coffee drinking, the most significant of which deal with the milieu into which its use was introduced. On the whole, however, it is rather vague, and seems to contain more than a bit of legend. Even Ibn 'Abd al-Ghaffār, reporting the whole affair, skeptically hedges in the final few sentences. By its very vagueness, in fact, it raises as many questions as it answers.

Concerning Dhabḥānī, we have some information from other sources, but this is disappointingly scanty.[10] Sakhāwī, the late fifteenth-century compiler of an important biographical dictionary, tells us that as a youth Dhabḥānī studied diligently and taught a bit, then became a Sufi, immersing himself in their mystical writings. He was a recluse, a man who only went out on Fridays or to see important people. He wrote many books, including works on Sufism. Information provided by Sakhāwī corroborates the date given for his death by Ibn 'Abd al-Ghaffār.[11] He makes no mention of Dhabḥānī's position as overseer of *fatwās* (a most unusual office), nor of his trip to Ethiopia and connection with coffee, though it is possible that even by the time of his death in 1497 Sakhāwī might not have heard of the drink. One cannot help but wonder, however, whether a man of such reputed hermitic propensities would have found any affair serious enough to make an expedition across the Red Sea to a strange land, unless we assume that this aspect of his nature only developed late in life.

In any event, what Dhabḥānī saw in Ethiopia, if indeed he went there, and what he did there and on his return to Yemen, are left open to doubt by Ibn 'Abd al-Ghaffār's account. To begin with, he found the people of Ethiopia "using" *qahwa* (*fa-wajada ahlahu yasta'milūna al-qahwa*). It is not clear from this whether the "use" of coffee by the Ethiopians was as a beverage, as those who took the habit from them later were to do, or whether they were eating the berries, as was occasionally seen, even in later times, in the Arabian Peninsula. A century and a half later, Kâtib Çelebi confirmed this practice: "Certain shaykhs, who lived with their dervishes in the mountains of Yemen, used to crush and eat the berries, which they called *qalb wabūn* [?], of a certain tree."[12] The phrase *yasta'milūna* ("they [were] using it") is suggestive, since the Arabic root most commonly associated with ingesting anything in a liquid form, or even as a gas (e.g., tobacco) is *sh-r-b*. We in the West may *take* coffee, but the Arab almost invariably *drinks* it.[13] On the other hand, the word *qahwa* tends to give the opposite impression. When the fruit of the coffee plant itself is referred to, one more often finds the term *bunn* used, generally for the whole berry, but often for the kernel of the berry as opposed to its husk (*qishr*). *Qahwa*, though, seems generally to be applied to a class of brewed beverages that contribute to wakefulness and are prepared in a specific way, though not necessarily from the same material. In any case, it would probably be a mistake here to expect too much specificity of vocabulary (especially since he "drinks" it when he falls ill in the Yemen). Consequently it is not clear whether at this very early stage coffee was consumed as a beverage, which was the first necessary step toward the development and popularity of coffeehouses.

The account also raises some questions concerning what might be called the natural history of the coffee plant. It is generally assumed that what we know as *coffea arabica* was not, in fact, native to the Arabian Peninsula, or at very least only a substandard variety was to be found there.[14] And yet, we have Dhabḥānī observing the people of Ethopia using coffee, though he did not know what its nature was, and only upon falling ill on his return to Aden did he try coffee. This leaves us with two alternatives: (*a*) for some reason he brought back a quantity of beans from Ethiopia, even though he lacked any personal experience with the fruit, or; (*b*) it had been growing native in Arabia all along, but had never been used for human consumption.

The medicinal benefits that Dhabḥānī is alleged to have derived from coffee are also spoken of in parallel accounts. Mouradgea D'Ohsson, writing in the eighteenth century, attributes the first use of coffee to a Sufi of Mocha (probably al-Shādhilī, who will be discussed shortly) who subsisted for some time in the desert on nothing else. Upon discovering that it was a cure for a sort of mange, some of al-Shādhilī's disciples returned to Mocha with news of its efficacy whereupon it soon became widespread.[15]

Jazīrī provides another account of the origins of coffee use, one that he attributes to a certain Fakhr al-Dīn Abū Bakr ibn Abī Yazīd al-Makkī, concerning a different Sufi shaykh, one of the order of the Shādhilīya.[16]

Fakhr al-Dīn al-Makkī said: "It has been said that the first to spread [the use of coffee] was al-Dhabḥānī, but what has reached us from a good many people is that the first one to introduce [*qahwa*] and to make [its use] a widespread and popular [custom] in the Yemen was our master,[17] Shaykh ... 'Alī ibn 'Umar al-Shādhilī, a pupil of our master, Shaykh ... Nāṣir al-Dīn ibn Maylaq, one of the masters of the shaykhs of the Shādhilīya order.... [It is said] that at first [*qahwa*] was made from *kafta*, that is, the leaves known as *qāt*, and neither from coffee beans nor from the husks [of that fruit]. [The use of this potion] continued to spread from region to region, until it came to the port of Aden the Protected. In Aden at the time of Shaykh ... al-Dhabḥānī there was no *kafta*, so he said to those who followed him and were dependent on him for guidance that 'coffee beans [*bunn*] [also] promoted wakefulness, so try *qahwa* made from it.' They tried it, and found that it performed the same function as [*qahwa* made from] *qāt*,[18] with little expense or trouble."

[Jazīrī continues:] The drinking of [*qahwa* made from *bunn*] continued to spread from its place of origin and other places, which we shall not waste the space to mention. There is no contradiction between the two statements ... since the former speaks of *qahwa* made from the husks [of the coffee berry], while the latter refers to *qahwa* from *qāt*.[19]

Since this passage presents a rather confusing range of uses of the word *qahwa*, perhaps this is the best place to discuss its derivation and use. *Qahwa* was a word in common use before coffee itself was known: it has a long pedigree as one of the epithets of wine. The Arabic root *q-h-w/y* denotes the idea of making something repugnant, or lessening one's desire for something. According to one medieval Arab lexicographer, *qahwa* is "wine, so named because it puts the drinker off his food; that is to say, it removes his appetite [for it]."[20] The application of this term to coffee was a simple step: just as wine removes one's desire for food, so coffee removes one's desire for sleep.[21] Of course, the application to coffee of a term originally denoting wine, for which according to some it was a wholesome substitute, and with which according to others it shared certain noxious and unholy characteristics, is indeed suggestive of a conscious attempt at association, though no contemporary writer known to us saw fit to point this out explicitly.[22] One may also consider the happy coincidence of the word *qahwa* with the place name Kaffa, a region in Ethiopia. It is possible that the berry or beverage was first called after Kaffa, and that subsequent to its introduction in Arabia those who knew of it there could not resist the poetical urge to apply to it a near-homophone that had been a term for wine. A third etymological explanation, that because of its effects in invigorating the body it was given a form derived from *quwwa* (strength or power), seems far less likely.[23]

The use of the word in the earliest times presents us with something of a problem. The two versions with which we are dealing use *qahwa* in quite different contexts. In the first version, the word *qahwa* seems to have already become synonymous with *bunn*, that is to say with the fruit of the specific plant, or with preparations made from it: Dhabḥānī sees the people of Ethiopia using *qahwa* (though we are not sure of the way in which they do this); he returns to Aden where he "drinks" it, and introduces "its drink" to his companions, and so forth. In the second version, *qahwa* seems to be more of a general type of preparation rather than one made of specific ingredients: the strictest definition the context allows is that it is a liquid, which we may assume is called by that name because of its sleep-inhibiting properties. The protagonist of this version, al-Shādhilī, is credited with introducing *qahwa*, but this is not made from the fruit of *coffea arabica* at all, but rather from *qāt*, a shrub whose highly stimulating leaves are still a popular addiction in the Yemen. It is Dhabḥānī's innovation of using coffee beans or husks that linked the idea of the general stimulating potion with the specific plant, so that soon the term *qahwa* precluded any other beverage. As a general rule, we can say that:

1. In common use the word *qahwa* came to be applied to the beverage made of the fruit of the *coffea arabica*.
2. The fruit itself is called *bunn*, while the two parts of the fruit, the kernel and the husk, are called *bunn* (or *ḥabb al-bunn*) and *qishr* respectively.
3. The word *qahwa* is sometimes modified to specify what sort of beverage we are speaking of, since it could be made from either the husks alone (*al-qahwa al-qishrīya*), from the kernels (*al-qahwa al-bunnīya*), or from a combination of the two, but it is restricted to those things made from the fruit of the coffee plant.

We know very little about the life of ʻAlī ibn ʻUmar al-Shādhilī. Neither the *Ḍaw' al-Lāmiʻ* of Sakhāwī nor the *Shadharāt al-dhahab* of Ibn al-ʻImād contains anything about him, and Jazīrī himself gives us next to no information about the man. Nonetheless, in the Mocha area at least, his name was always immediately linked to coffee. He was apparently something of a patron saint for the port town whose prosperity was so directly linked to coffee, as Carsten Niebuhr discovered in the eighteenth century.[24] When Niebuhr visited Yemen he was told that Shādhilī lived about four hundred years earlier, which would put him in the late fourteenth century. Most other evidence that we have for the introduction of coffee, including the eyewitness reports in Ibn ʻAbd al-Ghaffār's version, makes this date seem improbably early.[25]

A third tradition, which seems to be mentioned first by Najm al-Dīn al-Ghazzī, offers some tantalizingly suggestive information, but at the same time presents considerable difficulties.[26] It names another al-Shādhilī, one Abū Bakr ibn ʻAbd Allāh, known as al-ʻAydarūs, as the father of coffee:

In his travels, he passed by a coffee bush, and nourished himself, as is the custom of the pious,[27] on its fruit, which he found untouched, in spite of the fact that it was plentiful. He found that it made his brain nimble, and that it promoted wakefulness and stimulation for [the performance of] religious duties. So [he began] taking it for nourishment and food and drink, and he directed his followers to do so too, until [the practice] became widespread in the Yemen.

This account seems to combine a number of themes that we have seen before. Elements in it remind us of the three other reputed originators of the habit, the Shādhilī mentioned by D'Ohsson, ʻAlī ibn ʻUmar al-Shādhilī, and Dhabḥānī. The story of the discovery of coffee during his wanderings seems a common one: it is not only to be found in the Dhabḥānī story; it also appears in D'Ohsson's version, and is perhaps even closer to that one, since in both he nourishes himself completely on the bean. Yet D'Ohsson's Shādhilī is given the improbably early date of 1258 (A.H. 656). With ʻAlī ibn ʻUmar there is one interesting connection: both he and ʻAydarūs are associated with the name of the Sufi scholar Nāṣir al-Dīn ibn Maylaq (1330–95 [A.H. 731–97]).[28] ʻAlī ibn ʻUmar is believed to have been a disciple of his, while ʻAydarūs is said to be the direct heir, with a number of intermediaries, to his spiritual position.

The immediate temptation, when faced with a series of coincidental reports such as this, is to assume, especially in the case of the three Shādhilīs, that the sources have confused one for the other. Discarding the thirteenth-century Shādhilī as a highly unlikely candidate,[29] the other two seem to have so much in common that it is hard to imagine that they do not represent two traditions made from one. There seems to be adequate evidence to confirm the existence of 'Alī ibn 'Umar al-Shādhilī who died in the early fifteenth century and was a disciple of Ibn Maylaq. Further, Niebuhr tells us that the patron of the city of Mocha, who achieved this honor by being the father of the habit that became the economic lifeblood of the city, lived in the late fourteenth century. Moreover, while Fakhr al-Dīn al-Makkī's story of 'Alī ibn 'Umar, as it is related by Jazīrī, gives no dates for him, it would suggest that the man had introduced *qahwa* some time considerably before 1475. While it is possible that 'Aydarūs, who died in the first decade of the sixteenth century, cannot be completely eliminated by this statement, he is by far a less likely choice. Though it is not possible to rule out one or the other entirely, all the other evidence seems to point to an earlier introduction of coffee than is likely if we are speaking of 'Aydarūs. One other advantage is that the version from Jazīrī is the earlier, and Jazīrī, when not talking of matters of religious or legal controversy (which he could distort as well as anybody), seems a rather cautious, conservative scholar, not as quick as many to pass on whatever unsubstantiated morsels came his way.

When all the inconsistencies from these reports have been considered, and where those aspects of the reports containing contradictions that can be resolved neither by evidence nor reason have been set aside, there remain a number of general statements that can be made concerning the introduction of coffee into the lands of Islam:

1. In the first, second or, less likely, third quarter of the fifteenth century, a potion made from some stimulating vegetable matter seems to have gained

popularity among the adherents of certain Sufi orders in the Yemen. The use of this drink may very well have originated with a Sufi shaykh of the Shādhilīya order.

2. By some point in the third quarter of the fifteenth century, this beverage was being made from a part or parts of the coffee bean. This innovation is often attributed to the scholar and Sufi, Muḥammad al-Dhabḥānī, who died circa 1470–71. The introduction of coffee, if not the work of Dhabḥānī himself, was at least contemporaneous with his adult life.
3. It was first widely used in the Yemen.
4. Whatever other points of controversy may exist, its early use is almost always connected with Sufi orders.

The last two, more general statements, demand some attention. Concerning the connection with the Yemen, there remains very little to say. The proximity of Yemen to Ethiopia of course makes it quite understandable that there would be significant contact between the two regions, as well there had been, going back to the pre-Christian era. In addition, the climate of the Yemen (not of the Tihāma, the coastal plain, but of the mountains of the hinterland) was well suited for the cultivation of coffee, either as a native crop or one recently introduced. The connection of coffee to the Yemen in the minds of later authors was doubtless strengthened by the fact that until the early eighteenth century almost all coffee consumed in the Middle East (and Europe, for that matter) came from the ports of the Yemen, which served as outlets for the coffee growing areas of the interior.

The link between coffee and the various Sufi orders is one upon which our sources are unanimous, and this connection was one that was to have importance not only for its initial use in the Yemen, but also for its spread throughout the peninsula and to Egypt and Syria as well.

Sufism places its emphasis on the mystical reaching out for God—a God more personally intelligible than the stern, abstract diety of the orthodox scholastic. Its adherents regard it, in the ideal, as a searching for a state of complete obliviousness to the outside world, and a sort of spiritual merging with the divine, the attainment of a total severance from both mundane concerns, and from the five senses. Their *dhikr*s—the communal worship services usually held at night—are often marked by various practices designed to encourage a trancelike concentration on God, to the exclusion of all else; to attain, at least momentarily, the obliviousness that was sought. This they often try to effect by the rhythmic repetition, in unison, of a name or epithet of God, or perhaps of the *shahāda*, the basic Muslim profession of faith. Certain prescribed swaying of the head, hands, or entire body enhances the almost hypnotic effect of the chants.[30]

Members of some orders apparently did not turn only to such self-induced trances for their spiritual bliss. The use of various sorts of drugs as inducements to holy rapture was not unknown. Franz Rosenthal describes a hashish-eating ritual that one of his sources ascribes to a certain Shaykh Qalandar, who in conclusion warns against "divulging its benefits to the common people, instead of sharing it with fellow sufis."[31] It is not improbable that other drugs were used. Shādhilī, as we are told, made the invigorating potion *qahwa* from the leaves of the *qāt* shrub, which, by all acounts, is a particularly effective stimulant. Since their *dhikr*s were often held at night (most members of any order were not full-time holy men, but people who by day had to pursue their mundane crafts and vocations), anything that could lead them to mental excitement and ward off sleep would be seen as an aid to devotions. Jazīrī himself puts a great emphasis on this useful property of coffee. Though a legal scholar, he also seems to have had strong connections in Sufi circles, and was close to many of the mystical luminaries of his day.[32] He stresses constantly that while there were other benefits to be had from coffee, this aid in staying awake for pious purposes was the primary good (and, conversely, seeking its aid for frivolous pursuits was a perversion of the proper use of the beverage).[33] In the eyes of its earliest proponents, coffee was drunk not because it was thirst quenching, not because its taste was pleasing, but because of its physical effects. It is no wonder that among the claims made by its first enemies was that it had an intoxicating effect, since its mind-altering properties were precisely its major attraction.

The conclusion that coffee was first used in the central lands of Islam by Sufis in mid-fifteenth-century Yemen may seem merely to be argument *ex nihilo*, that because we do not find coffee mentioned in earlier sources, it was not known. If this were the case, the evidential underpinnings for such a finding would be very flimsy indeed, though often that is the only kind of information available in writing on the history of material culture. Jazīrī himself, in writing on the same subject, notes that one must be cautious of this pitfall. He cautions the reader that an item might be around for quite some time, but when something finally draws a writer's attention to it, he instantly assumes that it is a recent innovation, and traces its introduction to his own time.[34] Yet given a combination of admittedly *ex nihilo* evidence—up to this time we simply find no mention of coffee—and the eyewitness testimony of those who had reached maturity before the mid-fifteenth century and who have vivid memories of first seeing it used, we can at least say that all the evidence points to the mid-1400s.

There is, however, an alternate explanation. While it would perhaps be unjust to characterize the Yemen as a backwater, nonetheless it would be safe to say that it was not exactly at the center of the late medieval Islamic world, figuratively or literally. In particular there is a certain remoteness about the mountainous areas of the land, the areas where the cultivation of coffee was most likely to have met with success. It is not inconceivable that coffee may have been used for centuries in these isolated regions without word spreading to the outside. Even when the subject was well known and openly discussed, our Yemeni sources on the origins of coffee use come not from the mountains, but from such places as Zabīd in the Tihāma or Aden on the coast. Admitting this possibility, we can still retain part of our original conclusion: that the central fact in the introduction of coffee into a common urban context, and its spread to other areas of the Muslim world, was its adoption by Sufi groups in the larger cities of the Yemen. This, from all the available evidence, can be traced to the mid-fifteenth century.

THE SPREAD OF COFFEE TO THE ḤIJĀZ AND EGYPT

Members of Sufi orders were not as a rule reclusive, hermitic holy men. They went to their shops or workplaces, bargained in the markets, went to the baths, and went home at night to their families. This involvement of the members of the orders in everyday affairs of the world was, in all likelihood, one of the most important factors in the spread of coffee. If Sufism had been a movement that stressed isolation, a movement of high walls and cloisters such as so often characterized Christian monasticism, the use of coffee might have remained an arcane practice limited to the few who belonged. This was not, however, the case. If coffee was an aid to the *dhikr*, it could also be of assistance to the tedious activities of the workplace; if it could be prepared at the meeting place of the order, so could it be prepared by one's wife or servants at home. We have no direct evidence of how coffee came into general use in the Yemen outside the Sufi meeting, but conjecture along these lines is perhaps most fruitful.

Coffee was perhaps brought into other areas of the Arabian Peninsula by traders and others who traveled outside the Yemen who were also Sufis. Or perhaps it had become so generally familiar to those in the Yemen that almost any traveler from there might have known of it and used it. Whatever the case may be, we have more concrete dates once the spread began. In the early sixteenth century, Fakhr al-Dīn ibn Abī Yazīd al-Makkī writes: "And as for us, *qishr* reached us in Rey in Mecca and other places twenty or more years ago, but *qahwa* made from it did not spread until the end of the ninth [fifteenth] century."[35] This short passage gives us quite a bit to go on. It adds further fuel to the debate over the form in which coffee was used in the earliest times: first the husks appeared, and only later was *qahwa* made from them. Further, the passage establishes that coffee was introduced to Mecca sometime in the last decade or so of the fifteenth century. How and why coffee reached Mecca we do not know, but we do know, from a passage that will be discussed at length in the next chapter, that by 1511 (A.H. 917) its use was already well established there.

Ibn 'Abd al-Ghaffār gives us a much clearer picture of when, how, and by whom coffee was introduced to Cairo.[36] Sometime in the first decade of the tenth [sixteenth] century (*fī al-'ushr al-awwal min hādha al-qarn*), in the "Yemeni quarters" (*riwāq al-Yaman*) of the Azhar theological complex, coffee began to be drunk. The first to use it there "were mendicants, who were concerned with the performance of the meetings of *dhikr* and praise [of God] according to their previously mentioned Way." That is to say, it was being used by Sufis from the Yemen. Ibn 'Abd al-Ghaffār makes it clear that there was a certain amount of ceremony involved: the shaykh himself distributed the coffee to the participants during the *dhikr*, while they chanted.[37] Joining the Yemenis in this were others, probably Sufis as well, from Mecca and Medina. Nor were these meetings restricted to members of the order: others, who were merely present in these quarters, also drank with them. Soon it was being sold in the streets immediately around the mosque, and was drunk openly, not only in the precincts of the Azhar theological complex, but in much of the rest of Cairo.

By the first decade of the sixteenth century, then, coffee had spread from the Yemen to the Ḥijāz and Cairo. As we shall see in the next chapter, it was another decade or so before it reached Syria, probably via the pilgrimage caravan, and from there it was carried to Istanbul around the middle of the 1500s.

In the meantime, however, something else was happening that was to have a profound effect on the fortunes of coffee in the Islamic world. Once coffee had been taken out of the context of the Sufi *dhikr* and introduced into general consumption, it was embraced by an entirely different group of advocates, and with them the associations and images connected with the drink changed. While it remained one of the props of the nocturnal devotional services of the Sufis, others, perhaps less spiritually inclined, found it a pleasant stimulus to talk and sociability. From this the coffeehouse was born, and the controversy that was to surround this institution, and coffee itself by association, began to make itself heard.

CHAPTER 3

Coffee, Coffeehouses, and the Opposition

If we were to take the attitude expressed by the early proponents of coffee drinking at face value, nothing would have seemed more natural than the continued spread and popularity of this wholesome, beneficial, and indeed pious habit; and nothing more surprising than the opposition to it of those people (whom they dismissed as fanatics or self-serving hypocrites) who began to make their opinions known in the early sixteenth century. Jazīrī tells us:

> [After the spread of coffee to Egypt and its brisk consumption in the precincts of the Azhar] the situation continued along these lines: much coffee was drunk in the quarter of the mosque; it was sold openly in a multitude of places. In spite of the long time [that it had been drunk], not a soul gave any thought to interfering with coffee drinkers, nor did anyone find fault with the drink either in itself or because of factors [associated with but] external to it, such as passing the cup around and the like. All this was in spite of the fact that it had also become widespread in Mecca, and was drunk in the Sacred Mosque itself, so that there was scarcely a *dhikr* or observance of the Prophet's birthday (*mawlid*) where coffee was not present.[1]

The first case of attempted prohibition for which we have a detailed report took place in Mecca in 1511 (A.H. 917). We cannot, however, be as sure as Jazīrī that until this incident there had been no controversy surrounding coffee. Judging from the context of the report on the Meccan case itself, there had been questions for some time in many minds over the legal status of coffee.[2] It is, indeed, most unlikely that a step such as was taken in Mecca was not preceded by growing sentiment against coffee.

THE CASE OF 1511 AND SUBSEQUENT INCIDENTS IN MECCA

To the question of why the opposition to coffee arose at this particular time and place, one can offer only a few tentative suggestions. First, as we have seen, coffee had come into use only a relatively short time before, and even a shorter period had passed since its spread from the Yemen: no more than twenty years, and perhaps less than ten. Second, by the early sixteenth century, coffee had moved out of the Sufi meetings and into institutions where the emphasis was on pleasure rather than piety.

Before closely examining the events of the 1511 incident and their significance, we should first take a look at the sources for the affair. Aside from Jazīrī, there seems to be no other writer on coffee who has much to say on the incident, and mention of it is even lacking in such Meccan chronicles of the day as are available.[3] This is not as curious as it first appears, since such chronicles are generally concerned more with the doings of the notable families of the city than with those of petty Mamluk officials. Jazīrī, however, speaks at great length on the events of the case. The sources that he uses can be divided into two categories. Where he touches on the incident in the first chapter of his treatise, and in most of the second chapter, which is entirely devoted to it, he uses his usual sources (see Appendix) and gives his own interpretation of and opinions on what happened. In the first part of the second chapter, however, he reproduces (as he claims, "word for word") the official account, including what might be called the minutes (*maḥḍar*) of the council of prominent jurists at Mecca that gave a ruling on the question of coffee drinking. It is not entirely clear how Jazīrī got hold of this document. Not only did he spend most of his life in Cairo, (in spite of his peninsular origins), but since the *'Umdat al-ṣafwa* was written no earlier than 1556 (A.H. 963), he was probably too young to have been present at the meeting in 1511. Chances are he either copied these minutes as well from the work of Ibn 'Abd al-Ghaffār, who wrote circa 1530 (A.H. 937),[4] or he saw a copy of it on one of his many trips to Mecca, where he visited Sa'd al-Dīn 'Alī ibn Muḥammad ibn al-'Arrāq, a leading jurist of the time.[5] Whatever the case may be, he seems to have seen the actual document, or at least an accurate copy of it: he describes in detail the certifications of authenticity by and signatures of the jurists at its bottom. What is most important about this account is not merely that it gives a clear description of the events leading up to the attempt at prohibition, but that it is one of the earliest extant examples of polemic literature against coffee. According to Jazīrī, these minutes were drawn up by one Shams al-Dīn Muḥammad al-Ḥanafī, known as al-Khaṭīb, the *naqīb*[6] of the *qāḍī al-quḍāt* (chief judge) Sarī al-Dīn ibn al-Shiḥna. Jazīrī brands this Shams al-Dīn as one of the leading opponents of coffee in Mecca at that time. The text of the minutes certainly makes it clear enough that its author looked on coffee drinking with stern disapproval. The difference between Shams al-Dīn's "official" account and 'Abd al-Ghaffār's version preserved by Jazīrī is reflected not only in the tone, but in their factual content as well.

Concerning even those events that led to the convening of the council of jurists, there are considerable discrepancies between the two accounts. The "official" version begins by going to great lengths to establish the piety of the first principal opponent of coffee in Mecca, Khā'ir Beg al-Mi'mār, pasha of the Mamluks in Mecca and *muḥtasib* of the town.[7] On the eve of Friday, 20 June 1511 (23 Rabī' I 917), the account tells us:

> He performed the last evening prayers in the Sacred Mosque with companions, as was his habit. He then walked about the Ka'ba, as seemed proper to him, beginning and ending this act by kissing the Black Stone [set into the side of the Ka'ba . . .]. He then performed the prayers that accompany such circumambulations, and pronounced some more supplicatory prayers. Then he went and drank water from the spring of Zamzam, and prayed yet again.[8]

It was upon heading home from these devotions that he saw an assembly of some men with lanterns in one of the precincts of the mosque. They had, the report continues, been gathered by one Ḳorḳmāz (obviously a Mamluk), ostensibly for the celebration of the *mawlid* (birthday) of the Prophet. When he approached them, these men hurried to extinguish their lanterns, which made him increasingly suspicious of their activities. When he sought to investigate their actions, he learned that they were swallowing some drink "in the fashion of drinkers swallowing an intoxicant";[9] and in his capacity as *muḥtasib* saw it as his duty to suppress such a practice. Further, he learned that the drink they were using was called *qahwa*; it had become popular throughout Mecca, he was told, and was drunk in places "like taverns," where a variety of forbidden things went on. When he learned this, feeling it incumbent upon the believer to fight such things, he chastised those present, broke up their gathering and sent them on their way. The next morning he decided to convene a meeting of the leading ulema (religious scholars) of Mecca to take up the question of coffee.[10]

The Jazīrī/Ibn 'Abd al-Ghaffār version of what happened is significantly different. According to this account, the original impetus for the prohibition of coffee did not come from Khā'ir Beg himself. Two physicians of Persian origin, Nūr al-Dīn Aḥmad al-Kāzarūnī and his brother 'Alā' al-Dīn, were said to have goaded Khā'ir Beg into opposing coffee, with the help of the aforementioned Shams al-Dīn al-Khaṭīb.[11] It is probably these three Jazīrī means when he says, further on, that "they" represented the importance of taking such a step to Khā'ir Beg in exaggerated terms, suggesting that in so doing he should receive "great glory and abundant rewards."[12] They suggested to him that the beverage was endowed with all sorts of vile characteristics, and are said to have been instrumental in arranging for the council. As we shall see, their rôle in carrying the prohibition through continued during and after the meeting. What it would seem that we have here is a small but influential core of opponents of coffee, men of legal and medical background (or at least legal pretentions), who had been active for a time prior to this incident. What their original objections to coffee were we cannot say with certainty, since, when the time for action came, they employed almost any and every conceivable legal argument to effect their goals.

Jazīrī raises an additional objection to the official version that deserves some consideration. Khā'ir Beg was the *muḥtasib*, the inspector of markets, who not only looked after weights and measures and trade practices in general, but also was something of an arbiter of morals, whose duties included "forbidding reprehensible things." The office had come to combine something of the functions of the

Bureau of Consumer Affairs and the vice squad. Is it at all likely, asked Jazīrī, that one with these responsibilities would have been completely unaware of a practice that had been going on more or less openly for several years? Certainly the sudden discovery and righteous indignation when he learned of the consumption of the beverage would suggest such ignorance. It is far more likely that Jazīrī was right, that, along with the lengthy description of the scrupulous detail that Khā'ir Beg paid to his devotional exercises that night, what we have before us are mere rhetorical devices, hyperbole devised to emphasize the piety of the supposed initiator of action against coffee.

At any rate, on that Friday the council of leading Shāfi'ī, Mālikī, and Ḥanafī ulema was convened. Khā'ir Beg had coffee brought in in a large vessel (*mirkan*), though the purpose of this is not clear, since there is no mention of anyone actually tasting it during the proceedings. When asked for their opinion concerning coffee and the meetings held for the consumption of it, the jurists chose to deal with the meetings first. Considering the nature of these meetings and the activities associated with them, they decided that such gatherings were forbidden, and that it was incumbent upon anyone who had the power, to censure and suppress them. On this there was practically no discussion, though, as we shall see later in chapter eight, one poor soul had the audacity to argue a few points, and was consequently rebuked severely, and almost prosecuted.

The ulema were at first unwilling to allow this ban to be extended to coffee itself. On this question, they applied the principle of "basic permissibility" (*al-ibāḥa al-aṣlīya*), that is to say, that because all vegetation was originally created by God for the enjoyment of humankind, a comestible is permitted until it is demonstrated to have some attribute that would necessitate prohibition. If, they told Khā'ir Beg, it were found that coffee produced any harm to the body or mind, or if it produced intoxication, delight, or wanton amusement, it was forbidden:[13] the determination of this would have to rest with physicians.

This argument, apparently, had been anticipated by Khā'ir Beg. He immediately produced two doctors whom he had kept waiting in the wings—Nūr al-Dīn Aḥmad al-Kāzarūnī and 'Alā' al-Dīn—and asked them to give their opinions on the beverage. They told him that it was of a cold and dry nature, and, not surprisingly, that it was harmful to the well-balanced temperament. One of those present (whom the official report dismisses as a man "without the slightest bit of medical knowledge") raised the objection that the *Minhāj al-bayān* cited it as beneficial for drying up phlegmatic conditions.[14] The two physicians dismissed this argument by merely saying that the *Minhāj al-bayān* was referring to another plant altogether. At this juncture, several of those present stood to support the doctors: they said that, knowing that it was legal, they had drunk coffee, and had suffered mental and personality changes from the beverage.

All this Jazīrī regarded as pure sham. His opinion concerning the "independent witnesses" who came forth is, if anything, even worse than his opinion concerning the doctors. There were, he claims, only two of them, and they were the scum of the earth, men whose credibility was highly suspect, who had blatant ulterior motives for the testimony they gave.[15]

The jurists, however, apparently found nothing wrong with the witnesses or their testimony. Based on the medical evidence, they decided that coffee itself was forbidden. Khā'ir Beg, acting on this finding, had it proclaimed throughout Mecca that the sale and consumption, public or private, of coffee was prohibited, and that those who disregarded his ban would be punished. According to Jazīrī, he carried through with his threats: coffee was burned in the streets of Mecca, and many of those who trafficked in or consumed it were beaten. In the meantime, Shams al-Dīn al-Khaṭīb drew up the official account of the events and the minutes of the council. Several of the jurists who had been present certified the accuracy of the account at the bottom of the document. Shams al-Dīn, along with the two doctors, also drew up a legal question asking for the general prohibition of coffee, which they dispatched to the central authories in Cairo along with a copy of the minutes.

Jazīrī all along suspects the jurists who gave this ruling against coffee of a certain amount of legal dishonesty. He claims many of them were coffee drinkers themselves; men who, had they not had ulterior motives, had they acted strictly in accord with what they knew the nature of coffee to be through personal experience, should have found it licit. He depicts them as acting under coercion: fearing the wrath of Khā'ir Beg, and knowing how fanatical he was on the subject, they dared not issue a ruling contrary to what they very obviously knew his wishes to be.

In any event, the attempt to ban coffee was doomed from the start. The official decree arrived some time later from Cairo, but, while it echoed the original disapproval of the social gatherings for coffee drinking, it failed to prohibit the drink itself. Word of this leaked out to the general public (some of whom likely had continued the habit secretly all the time), and coffee once again was consumed in the open. The official snub apparently knocked some of the enthusiasm out of Khā'ir Beg, and he no longer saw any point in pursuing the suppression of coffee.

It is, in passing, curious that the main protagonists in the Meccan drama all subsequently suffered official disgrace. Khā'ir Beg was removed from the governorship in 1512 (A.H. 918), replaced by the Amīr Ḳuṭlubāy. This in itself might be attributed to the usual insecurity of official tenure in the Mamluk system. Shams al-Dīn al-Khaṭīb's fate is far more interesting. In 1512, 'Alā' al-Dīn ibn al-Imām, the overseer of the private domain of the sultan (*nāẓir al-khawāṣṣ al-sharīfa*), arrived in Mecca on business. Part of his business, it seems, was to strip Shams al-Dīn of his public functions and privileges, and to have him carried back to Cairo. From this latter intention he was dissuaded, but Shams al-Dīn, out of chagrin, kept to his house for months afterward. Finally he joined up with a caravan going to Cairo, but died on the way, at Yanbū'.[16] The physicians eventually met an even more unpleasant fate, although it also seems connected in no way with the events of 1511. The two emigrated to Cairo where, after the 1517 Ottoman conquest of the city, Selim I, "for reasons known best to God," had them cut in two at the waist in a manner popular among the Mamluks.[17]

Mecca was the scene as well of a serious incident involving coffee in 1525–26 (A.H. 932).[18] In that year, Muḥammad ibn al-'Arrāq, a jurist of considerable reputation, came to Mecca.[19] It reached him shortly thereafter that all sorts of reprehensible things (*munkarāt*) were going on in the coffeehouses of the town. Because of these things, he directed the officials to close these places down. Here it is clear that coffeehouses, and the activities therein, were the targets of opposition, not coffee itself: Ibn al-'Arrāq affirmed the legality of coffee, and took no steps to prohibit it. In Medina, where he had lived earlier, he had long been acquainted with coffee, but had shown no predisposition toward banning it. In one case brought before him concerning coffee, his ruling was unfavorable, but it was the circumstances peculiar to the case, not the drink itself, which drew his disapproval: there was a woman in the town who had been going around, unveiled, selling coffee. At first he forbade her to continue with her trade, then he relented, stipulating only that she keep covered at all times.[20]

At any rate, Muḥammad ibn al-'Arrāq died the following year, and, if they had not already done so, the coffeehouses then reopened. His successors, it is quite clear, had no desire whatsoever to suppress in any way the use of the drink. His son, Sa'd al-Dīn 'Alī, not only approved of the drink, but served it openly to guests.[21]

This seems to have been the last major affair involving the prohibition of coffee in the Ḥijāz, with the exception of one peculiar incident. During the pilgrimage of 1544 (A.H. 950), the caravan from Damascus brought word that, by order of the Ottoman sultan, coffee was forbidden, and those who sold it were to refrain from doing so. This is one of the earliest indications of the Ottoman government's awareness of the existence of coffee, and of the legal questions surrounding it.[22] This action was brought about, according to unnamed sources, by the complaints of a Turkish woman, who had previously lived in Mecca.[23] There is no mention of what it was specifically she objected to, whether it was coffeehouse activity, or the consumption of coffee in the sacred precincts of the mosque, or the drink coffee itself. At any rate, the Meccans were not about to let a decree from Istanbul cheat them of their by now well-established pleasures. The prohibition was observed for all of about a day, Jazīrī tells us, and then things returned to normal.

EARLY OPPOSITION IN CAIRO

Coffee spread to Cairo early in the sixteenth century through the Azhar, to which Yemenīs and Ḥijāzīs had carried their habit. It was from the Azhar again that the opposition to coffee in Cairo first came, opposition that was not merely an inconvenience to the many who had acquired the habit, but that actually led to considerable civil disturbance and fighting in the streets. The principal in this incident was one Aḥmad ibn ʿAbd al-Ḥaqq al-Sunbāṭī (d. 1547 [A.H. 954]), a Shāfiʿī scholar and preacher at the Azhar. His father (d. 1524–25 [A.H. 931]) had been an early opponent of coffee, and had issued a *fatwā* against it.[24] As the report has it, in 1532–33 (A.H. 939) Aḥmad ibn ʿAbd al-Ḥaqq al-Sunbāṭī was asked: "What do you think ... of a drink that they call *qahwa*, which they gather about and drink, and which they claim is allowed, in spite of the fact that many wicked things spring from it: is it permitted or forbidden?"[25] Sunbāṭī answered that it was prohibited. He wrote a long response based on the information of those who had drunk it and then repented, and on what was told him of the gatherings in coffeehouses. His opposition to the beverage became quite well known: he is considered something of the father of the anti-coffee faction in Cairo, as Yūnus al-ʿAythāwī al-Shāfiʿī (d. 1570 [A.H. 978]) (author of several treatises on the subject) was in Damascus. Many of the men of religious learning followed his initial lead on this question.[26]

Others, more inclined to action than reflection, followed Sunbāṭī as well. In 1534–35 (A.H. 941), he delivered several fierce harangues on the subject. A group, provoked by the strength of the sermons, set out (according to Jazīrī, on their own, a mere mob of rowdies without official sanction) and attacked several coffeehouses, smashed the fixtures, and beat many of those they found there. The proponents of coffee took to the streets, and the threat of civil violence was such that the question was brought before Muḥyi al-Dīn Muḥammad ibn Ilyās, a Ḥanafī judge in Cairo at the time.[27] Seeking the advice of a group of Cairene ulema, he finally sided with those who thought it legal. He also seems to have adopted an experimental approach to his investigation of the question: he held a council where he offered coffee to those present, and observed them, trying to detect any signs of intoxication or other mental effects. Finding none, he ruled in favor of coffee. In spite of the considerable respect in which he was held by scholars of his time, Sunbāṭī was subjected to the merciless poetic satire that is the customary lot of one whose decision, unpopular with the literati, is overturned by a higher authority.[28]

Cairo's coffeehouses were the targets as well of an incident in January-February 1539 (Ramaḍān 945). Coffeehouses were particularly popular in this month of fasting, doing very brisk business at night. Thus they were probably fairly crowded when, one night, the commander of the night watch (*ṣāḥib al-'asas*) swept down on them, and had those whom he found there ignominiously dragged off, some tied up, and some in irons. It is unclear if he was acting under command from a higher authority, or whether the raid was entirely of his own planning. The prisoners spent the rest of the night in custody, after which they each received seventeen lashes apiece and were released. Fear of a repetition of such a raid seems to have counted for very little: after a few days, the coffeehouses were again operating normally.

THE NATURE OF THE EARLY OPPOSITION

Several general statements can be made concerning these early attempts at prohibition. The first, most obvious, and least controversial is that none of them met with success. While not all edicts against coffee or coffeehouses were overturned by official proclamation, as happened in Mecca in 1511, nonetheless there is a consistent pattern of failure for such efforts. The governments involved were unable to force on the populace edicts that proscribed the already deeply rooted habit of coffee drinking, and assemblies for that ostensible purpose. It is telling that there are repeated accounts of attempted suppression—which never had more than transitory success—in the same cities. Such a pattern of official impotence in the control of contraband had earlier parallels in Egypt and Syria. Even the effort to suppress the consumption of so obviously illegal a commodity as wine had to be repeated every few years, and clearly had little effect on actual practice. One can hardly read a score of pages from contemporary chronicles without coming across another account of the Mamluk sultan trying once again to close down the taverns.[29] Coffee, a beverage whose legal status was, at worst, ambiguous, was an even less likely target. One would have been hard pressed to find a jurist who would support the legality of wine—to do so would have been tantamount to apostasy—but on the subject of coffee, the religious community was clearly divided. Lacking both popular support and the unanimous approval of the men of religion, there was very little hope of success.

The second point to be made about these early prohibitions is that, far from starting off as an issue solely of interest to the religiously inclined who sought to express their alarm over this new habit, it was, from the first, a matter with which the civil authorities were very much concerned. The Ottoman government in 1544, the commander of the night watch in 1539, and, most obviously, Khā'ir Beg in 1511 all interested themselves in the question. To draw too sharp a line between political and religious concerns is perhaps a mistake: in theory at least, all aspects of human activity fall into the realm of the *sharī'a*, the holy law. Nonetheless, it would be foolish to ignore the fact that concern for the strict adherence of the believers to holy law was not always the sole anxiety of the governing powers. That Jazīrī tries to paint Khā'ir Beg as the misguided dupe of religious fanatics and not the mastermind of the movement is of little importance here. The official version, as Shams al-Dīn al-Khaṭīb and others presented it, begins not with the growing religious concern over the effects of coffee—concern which had doubtless been present for some time—but with Khā'ir Beg's alarm and suspicion over a meeting that he stumbled across one evening.

This point perhaps brings us to the question that lies at the heart of the matter, and which can serve as a starting point for the discussion of the social importance of coffee. Since, from the first, the opposition to coffee came from both the secular authorities and religious quarters—official and nonofficial—can we trace some common underlying principle to explain what was happening? Were there objections, not explicitly raised because they did not fall clearly within the context of the law, that were actually at the root of this opposition?

To pursue such questions, it is first necessary to realize that in attributing motives to the actions of the protagonists we must discern three distinct levels of interpretation: those motives explicitly voiced by the protagonists themselves; those that are attributed to them by the narrators and commentators; and finally, those that we feel are suggested by the circumstances surrounding the incidents and the actions of the protagonists themselves. These last are perhaps the most promising—we are, after all, chiefly interested in why these things happened, not in the explanation or rationalizations of the actors or their critics. At the same time, they must be approached with the most caution. It is dangerous enough to pay too much attention to the nearly contemporary, if admittedly hostile, commentaries of the likes of Ibn 'Abd al-Ghaffār or Jazīrī. We must admit that they have their own biases, and employ their interpretations with corresponding judiciousness. When, at a distance of four centuries and perhaps a more awesome cultural divide as well, we start to formulate theories of *why* they acted as they did, we must approach our own task with a healthy skepticism, not so much of our sources, but of our own judgment.

If we analyze what happened in Mecca in 1511 on these three levels, what we are presented with looks something like this:

1. The explicitly stated motives of the actors themselves: "We did it because: (*a*) at the gatherings the coffee drinkers behave in a reprehensible way; and (*b*) the stuff itself is bad for you, and therefore must be probihited."
2. The hostile commentators: "The principals in the drama acted out of sheer fanaticism (*ta'aṣṣub*), while the jurists, who should have known better, were so afraid of Khā'ir Beg that they dared not rule contrary to his wishes."
3. Our own synthesis: "In addition to all the other factors mentioned, which are probably all valid, we also notice that what first seems to have alarmed Khā'ir Beg—and well it should have—was the very idea of these clandestine nocturnal gatherings."

In trying to discern a pattern in all this, to extract general themes from the multitude of arguments and charges, it is probably wisest to discuss briefly the unconstructive sniping of the critical commentators, and then to discard this name calling, at least for the moment. The "minority report" of Jazīrī and Ibn 'Abd al-Ghaffār calls into question the purported motives of the principals, but offers little of substance to help us understand exactly what was happening. According to this account, the jurists who gave the decisions against coffee were motivated by fear and a desire to please Khā'ir Beg, in spite of their knowledge concerning the true nature of coffee. Khā'ir Beg himself acted out of a desire to attain a reward—in this world or the next—for his good works, which in this case consisted of suppressing an evil. Both this desire and the means by which it might be effected owe their inception to the conspiratorial triumvirate—Shams al-Dīn al-Khaṭīb, Nūr al-Dīn al-Kāzarūnī, and his brother 'Alā' al-Dīn. They, like all other opponents of coffee, acted out of what Jazīrī condemns as fanaticism (*ta'aṣṣub*). Exactly what he means by this is unclear, but lacking any other indication, we can infer from his use of the word that it means broadly "a conviction, not based on any specific and authoritative texts but rather on an exaggerated sense of piety—perhaps hypocritical—that there is something inherently wicked in coffee and coffee drinking (or in anything from which others seem to derive pleasure), and that therefore one must strive to suppress it." Any means to achieve that end, even knowingly giving distorted testimony, is viewed as justified. But Jazīrī's analysis of the situation stops with the idea of *ta'aṣṣub*: why some people had this overwhelmingly hostile, basically insupportable antipathy to coffee, or whether they had any ulterior motives reflecting an even deeper hypocracy, are matters he does not consider. His main goal here, as it is throughout his work, is to demonstrate that the arguments against coffee are invalid.

Concerning our own interpretations, we should here only briefly discuss those intimations that are not explicitly mentioned but are to be inferred from the accounts: such a detailed analysis of the texts will form the core of many of the subsequent chapters, and therefore will be referred to as the questions with which they deal arise. Here only one thing needs to be pointed out: all questions of religious law aside, Khā'ir Beg's attention was first attracted, and his sense of danger first aroused, by the mere sight of a group gathered around some lanterns in a part of the Sacred Mosque at Mecca. In those first few moments he knew nothing (if we are to believe the official account) of coffee or coffeehouses, of mental or physical harm, or of intoxication. He knew only of a gathering, and this in itself was sufficient to cause alarm. We find an inherent suspicion (and, considering their always vulnerable position, a natural and healthy one) on the part of the civil authorities concerning the rôle of coffee and the coffeehouse in encouraging extended social intercourse. This is a theme that will be seen to recur often throughout the sixteenth and seventeenth centuries.

Just as the jurists did in the Meccan case, it is clear from all that has been said that we must consider the prohibition of coffee as two separate questions: the legal question concerning coffee itself as a substance; and the socio-legal question, whether there are any factors associated with but external to coffee drinking that are socially undesirable. Jazīrī himself recognized this distinction. He was an outspoken advocate of coffee, as long as it was free from the taint of reprehensible actions; activities of the sort that had become common in the coffeehouses of the time were to his mind quite clearly indefensible. This is not an artificial distinction, but one that arises naturally from the arguments.

CHAPTER 4

Wine, Coffee, and the Holy Law

At first glance, it might not seem so terribly odd that some early attempts to forbid the use of coffee were based on the claim that it fell into the category of beverages prohibited by Islamic law. While not an intoxicant like wine, coffee does indeed possess some noticeably stimulating properties, and can have profound effects, both mental and physical, on the drinker. If wine and other drinks were prohibited because of their mind-altering characteristics, might not the same principle be applied, though admittedly with some hesitation, to coffee as well?

THE ISLAMIC PROHIBITION OF WINE

Coffee, clearly, is not mentioned in the Qur'ān. The only way that one could set about proving that it falls into the category of illicit beverages is to draw the analogy between the effects of coffee and those of wine. To do this, however, we first must have a firm understanding of the regulations concerning wine, and the principles that govern the legal status of other beverages.

While in certain fields—penal law, for example—there remain considerable gaps in the legal system, in other areas the centuries of commentaries, extrapolations, and codifications have served to clarify the religious and moral precepts originally given the believers through Muḥammad, and to broaden in some respects and limit in others the interpretation of these principles. To demonstrate how extension and limitation were often applied to the same question, we need look no further than the subject at hand—beverage laws.

As is the case with its treatment of so many other subjects, the Qur'ān expresses various, sometimes mutually incompatible, attitudes toward wine. It is harmful and beneficial; it is an abomination, a tool of Satan, yet it is one of the delights of Paradise promised the faithful. How these incompatibilities arose need only detain us for a short time. A traditional explanation has it that one of Muḥammad's more zealous companions (and later [634–44] caliph), 'Umar ibn al-Khaṭṭāb, seeing that wine was at the root of certain undesirable activities within the community, repeatedly asked the Prophet for "clarification"—that is to say, he asked that wine be forbidden.[1] Each time, the answer came not as a statement from Muḥammad, but as a revelation through him from God. Each time the revelation was stronger, but each time ways were found to circumvent it. Finally, God sent a revelation clearly forbidding wine.

It should offer little surprise that rivers of wine "delicious to the drinkers" (Qur'ān 47:15) should be promised the believers as one of the rewards of their steadfastness. In the relatively parched environment of central Arabia, where clear water was as cherished as it was rare,[2] such an image could not have helped but make a vivid impression on the listener. Wine, in its strictest sense, was not unknown to the Arabs of the Ḥijāz, though undoubtedly it was a rare import from the north. A far more common beverage in central Arabia was date wine, while in the Yemen a sort of mead (*bit'*) enjoyed wide popularity.[3]

At some point after Muḥammad's flight to Medina in 622, there is a shift in the attitude toward wine in the Qur'ān. At first it can be detected in a fairly innocent verse in which specific beverages are not even mentioned. Believers are merely enjoined from going to prayers when drunk, "so that you may know what you are saying" (Qur'ān 4:43)—certainly a reasonable enough request. Later they are warned that in wine and *maysir* (a sort of game played for stakes, see Glossary) there is both harm and benefit for mankind, but that the harm is the greater of the two (Qur'ān 2:219).[4] Finally, the prohibition of wine is totally affirmed:

> O you who believe, indeed *khamr* and *maysir* and stone idols and arrows of divination are abominable, the work of Satan, so shun them [so that] you might prosper. Verily Satan wishes through *khamr* and *maysir* to sow enmity and hatred among you, and to turn you from mention of God and from prayer. So are you among those who desist? (Qur'ān 5:90–91)

These three verses, and a mass of sayings attributed to Muḥammad (many of questionable authenticity) were the raw material from which the later codifiers of the law fashioned the regulations concerning beverages. As we shall see, the four distinct but mutually tolerant Sunnī schools of jurisprudence (*madhhab*, pl. *madhāhib*), interpreted these guidelines rather differently. What each school did, however, was to synthesize a body of laws which:

1. determined that the beverage known in the Arabic of the Qur'ān as *khamr* (translated here as "wine" more for ease than accuracy) was not only to be avoided, but that the Qur'ānic text meant that it was absolutely forbidden;

2. determined just what sorts of beverages fell under the rubric *khamr* and what sorts of beverages were not *khamr*;
3. fixed the corporal punishment to be inflicted on those who disobeyed this command of God, and determined the circumstances in which the punishment was to be administered.

The most obvious case of extension and limitation of the original precepts is found in the law of the Ḥanafī school of jurisprudence. In their interpretation, *khamr* means several different beverages, but can be applied to only those beverages specifically. Even the other schools, whose interpretation of *khamr* is much broader, consciously or unconsciously limit its application. Their principle, that all things that produce intoxication are prohibited, obviously admits a number of substances that are not strictly speaking wine. It is, however, still limited by the legal definition of intoxication. If coffee falls within the letter, or even the spirit, of laws concerning *khamr*, then we need look no further for an explanation of the considerable pious opposition to its use. If, however, it does not, then the source of the objection must be sought elsewhere.

In spite of the seeming clarity of Qur'ān 5:90–91, these verses became the focus of considerable controversy in the subsequent centuries, as the corpus of laws gradually evolved. The controversy centered mainly on how *khamr* was to be defined, and whether other beverages, though not strictly covered by the term *khamr*, were to be included in the prohibition. One can formulate a basic statement, the lowest common denominator, as it were, with which almost all scholars of the four major Sunnī schools of jurisprudence would agree. A certain substance, known as *khamr*, is clearly forbidden by the Qur'ān, and its consumption by Muslims is an offense that necessitates earthly, as well as eternal, punishment. This prohibition is so obviously established in Qur'ān 5:90–91, so clear-cut, that to claim that *khamr* is legal would be a denial of the validity of a Qur'ānic verse, and hence apostasy.[5] And yet, even on this basic principle, there were those who dissented. Ibn Qutayba mentions an "insolent and corrupt group of speculative philosophers," who claimed that in the verse God did not explicitly forbid *khamr*, but merely suggested, admittedly with some force, that one should desist from using it.[6] God, they said, made this as a suggestion for proper behavior, just as he suggested, without making it a strict obligation, that one make a contract for the manumission of a slave if one believes there to be any good in him (Qur'ān 24:33). If, they argued, God wished to prohibit *khamr* entirely, he would have said, "*Khamr* is prohibited," just as he said, "Carrion, blood, and pork are forbidden you" (Qur'ān 2:173).[7] According to Sarakhsī, some of the Mu'tazila (q.v., Glossary) conceded that *khamr* was forbidden, but only such quantities as would effect the goals of Satan: enmity and hatred within the community. Thus, they suggested that taking a small amount of it did not bring about these results, and so was legal.[8] Such opinions, however, were most certainly exceptional.

All four schools forbid the sale of *khamr* by or to Muslims, and since it is not property that a Muslim can legally possess, the destruction or theft of one's *khamr* by another does not necessitate restitution to the injured party in either money or kind.[9] Its use for any medicinal, cosmetic, nutritive, or economic end is strictly forbidden. The Ḥanafīs allow its use in cases of immediate danger of death, to keep one from perishing from dehydration or choking.[10] It is considered a "gross pollutant" (*najāsa ghalīẓa*), so that even a tiny amount soiling one's garment nullifies any prayers made while wearing the garment.

From this point of general agreement, however, the schools take up significantly differing positions. Actually, the Shāfiʿīs, Mālikīs, and Ḥanbalīs agree in all the essentials, and the main principle is not terribly complicated. Any amount of any beverage that, when taken in large quantities, will produce intoxication is forbidden. Some claim quite simply that any such beverage is *khamr*. Others stop short of this, but maintain that intoxicants that are not strictly *khamr* are to be placed in the same class with it for the purposes of the law. Consumption of any amount of these beverages leaves the offender open to the prescribed corporal punishment, either forty or eighty stripes.[11] These legal passages are usually quite short, since the principle, once established, is simple enough and broadly applicable. As we shall see further on, however, the application of this all-encompassing prohibition depends on: (1) the definition of what constitutes a large quantity; and (2) the definition of intoxication.

Ḥanafī law—and this is of primary interest to us because the Ḥanafī *madhhab* became the official school of the Ottoman state—differs considerably from the other schools on the subject of beverages.[12] Four beverages are prohibited by law:

1. *khamr*, that is to say, raw grape juice that has been allowed to ferment and become potent;
2. such a beverage made of grape juice that has been cooked, of which more than one-third of the original volume remains;
3. (uncooked) intoxicants made from dates;
4. (uncooked) fermented infusions of raisins.[13]

Infusions (*nabīdhs*) of raisins and dates are permitted if they have been cooked even the slightest amount (before fermentation), even if they then ferment and become alcoholic. One must only drink them in amounts that one believes will not make him drunk, and without [the intention of] "entertainment or wanton diversion." In like manner, *nabīdhs* of honey (*bit'*), wheat, barley, figs, or millet are all legal, even if they have not been cooked. Finally, *muthallath*, grape juice that has been cooked so that at least two-thirds of its original volume has boiled away (and one-third remains), which is then allowed to ferment, is legal.

The routes taken by the Ḥanafīs on the one hand, and the Shāfi'īs, Mālikīs, and Ḥanbalīs on the other, obviously lead them to very different destinations, although all schools rely on the same types of evidence, of which in this case there are two. The first is analogy, the attempt to determine if there is some underlying principle embodied in the idea of *khamr* that would allow or necessitate the prohibition of all intoxicants. The Ḥanafīs, of course, maintain a very strict definition: *khamr* is uncooked grape juice that has fermented. Advocates of a broader application of the term, on the other hand, rely on a bit of ad hoc etymology. *Khamr*, they claim, is derived from the verbal form *khāmara* (to seize, grasp, overwhelm), and is properly applied to anything that seizes or overwhelms the mind (*mā khāmara al-'aql*), that is, all intoxicants.[14] With this the Ḥanafīs take issue on several grounds. First, they question the etymology itself. *Khamr*, they argue, may come from an entirely different paradigm for the root *kh/m/r*, and does not necessarily carry with it the ideas of "seizing" or "overwhelming." Second, even if one admits that it does indeed come from *khāmara*, they maintain that one cannot necessarily apply such a specific epithet to all things that share a common characteristic. One calls a horse that is half white and half black "piebald," they would argue, but one cannot properly apply this term to a similarly colored garment. They assert that *khamr* has a very specific meaning upon which scholars of the Arabic

PLATES

PLATE 1

A late seventeenth-century engraving of a coffee tree from LaRoque's *Voyage de l'Arabie heureuse*. (Courtesy of the Library of Congress, Division of Rare Books)

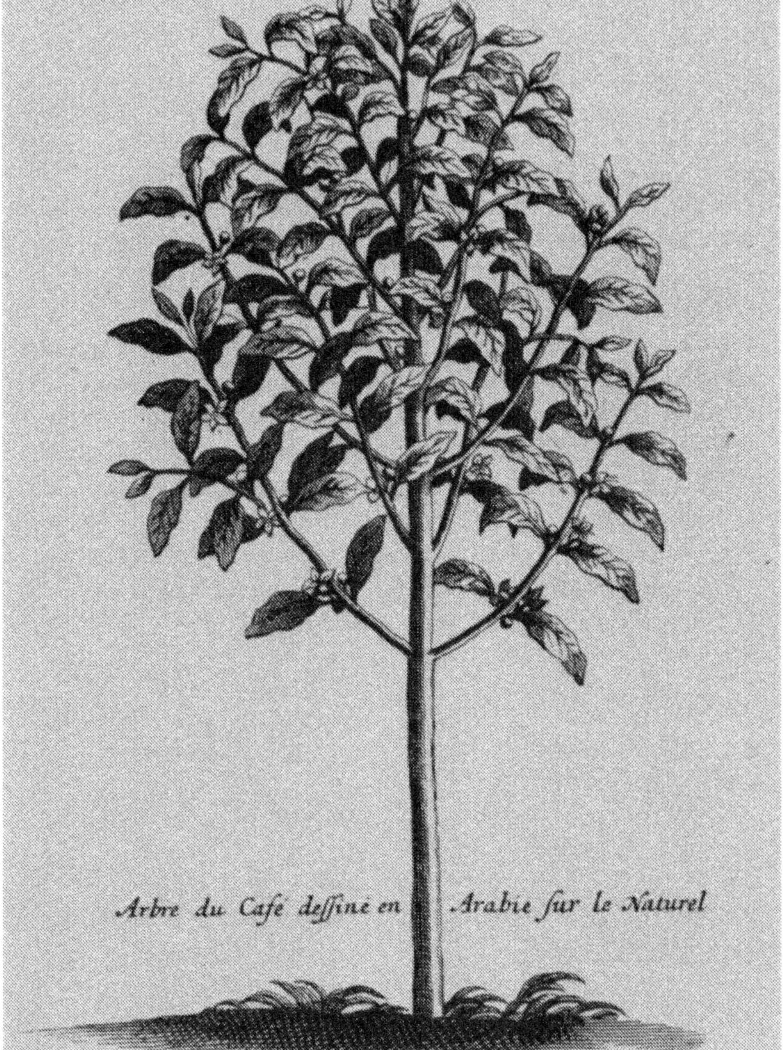

Arbre du Café dessiné en Arabie sur le Naturel

PLATE 2

This engraving of the branch of a coffee plant, includes depictions *below right to left*, of the matured coffee fruit on the stem, a detail of the fruit, both whole and in cross-section (note the separate husk and kernel), and the separated kernel. European interest in coffee in the sixteenth and seventeenth centuries, far from being limited to coffee as an imported commodity, focused as well on botanical considerations. This interest was not always purely scientific: at about the same time that this engraving was made, LaRoque's compatriots were trying, with eventual success, to cultivate the plant for commerical purposes in the Caribbean. (LaRoque, *Voyage*. Courtesy of the Library of Congress, Division of Rare Books)

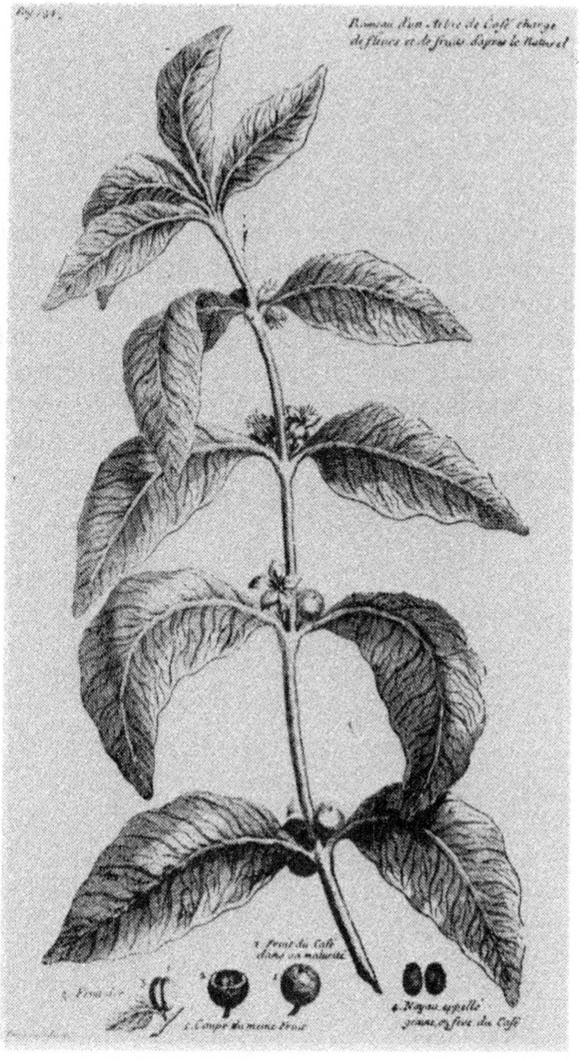
Rameau d'un Arbre de Café chargé
de fleurs et de fruits d'après le Naturel
1. Fruit du Café
dans sa maturité
2. Coupe du meme Fruit
4. Noyau appellé
graine, ou fève du Café

PLATE 3

The image of coffee in seventeenth-century Europe is depicted here by a seated Turk holding a rather oversize cup with the classical *ibrīq* by his knee. *Below right* is a branch from a coffee plant with beans, and *below left*, a coffee mill. Already used in parts of the Near East in preference to the mortar and pestle, the mill pictured here closely resembles those still widely seen in Turkey today. (Dufour, *Traitez nouveaux*)

Briq ou Pot Pour Faire Cuire
Plante du Café
Instrument Pour Torrefier le Cafe
Feves de Cafe

Plate 4

Upper left is a coffee pot designed by Nicolas de Blegny (1642?–1722); the others are types that were commonly seen in Europe in the late seventeenth century. Coffee was for the most part introduced to Europe by Christians from the Near East, usually Armenians or Greeks, who began by using the apparatus they brought with them. As is obvious from these pictures, however, within a few decades of being introduced to coffee, Europeans were designing new types of vessels to prepare the drink, and eventually developed new methods as well. (Blegny, *Le bon usage du thé, du caffé*. Courtesy of the Library of Congress, Division of Rare Books)

1re fig.

2e fig.

PLATE 5

Aside from the fact that early coffee cups were generally made of earthenware or porcelain, accounts differ as to their size and design. Some European engravings depict cups as large or larger than the typical mug today, but by most accounts the cups were indeed the same diminutive size as the standard Turkish coffee cup of the present. The design seems more akin to that of traditional handleless "Arab" coffee cups. (Blegny, *Le bon usage du thé, du caffé*. Courtesy of the Library of Congress, Division of Rare Books)

G

PLATE 6

This Turkish miniature from the mid-sixteenth century depicts, in a compressed space, a wide range of the activities common to the coffeehouse. Across the top, the usual business of the coffeehouse is conducted. Patrons enter on the left, while those who have already arrived, obviously men of no small rank, are seated center, drinking coffee from small porcelain cups. On the right, the *kahveci* prepares fresh coffee. The literary activity of the coffeehouse is shown in the central third of the miniature. The patrons seated on a low sofa, are reading aloud or to themselves, or are engaged in discussion. At the bottom, we find the more frivolous and disreputable pastimes. The musicians on the left, playing on stringed or percussion instruments and singing, provide the live entertainment. Other patrons are engaged in a variety of games, notably backgammon(center) and manqala(right). (Manuscript 439, folio 9. Courtesy of the Trustees of the Chester Beatty Library)

PLATE 7

This early nineteenth-century engraving by Antoine Melling (1763–1831) entitled *Intérieur d'un café publique sur la place de Tophane* is a particularly good depiction of a grand coffeehouse in the traditional arrangement. The patrons are seated on well-upholstered divans around the periphery of a large room, with a fountain in the middle. Far from being the dregs of society reported by some early European travelers, the patrons depicted here, seem all to be men of some stature, although on this point we do not really know how much must be attributed to the imagination of the artist. (Melling, *Voyage pittoresque de Constantinople*, plate 26. Courtesy of the General Research Division, The New York Public Library, Astor, Lenox and Tilden Foundations)

PLATE 8

In this detail from the previous engraving by Melling, the *kahveci* works with a pair of bellows, bringing a pot to boil in the cooking area, which is set off from the main salon of the coffeehouse. Note the various size pots, ranging from those that could accommodate only a few servings to those of considerably greater capacity. This would seem to corroborate the testimony of those who mentioned large pots or even caldrons in which coffee was prepared. (Melling, *Voyage pittoresque de Constantinople*. Courtesy of the General Research Division, The New York Public Library, Astor, Lenox and Tilden Foundations)

PLATE 9

This early nineteenth-century engraving by Thomas Allom (1804-72) entitled *Interior of a Turkish Caffinet* depicts a particularly ornate coffeehouse; the arrangement of seats is similar to that of plate 7. In this engraving, as in Melling's, the patrons are smoking tobacco from a variety of devices, including the familiar water pipe (*nargile*), and the long-stemmed *çubuk*, which from most accounts appeared much earlier than the water pipe. Note as well the entertainer on the extreme right, a story-teller accompanying himself on some sort of stringed instrument, probably akin to a *saz*. (Robert Walsh, *Constantinople*)

Plate 10

Even in the generally more severe climate of Istanbul, outdoor cafés enjoyed considerable popularity whenever the weather permitted. This 1839 engraving by William Bartlett (1809–54), entitled *Coffee Kiosque, on the Port*, depicts a waterside coffeehouse in Istanbul on the Golden Horn, near where the navy yard is today. (Julia Pardoe, *The Beauties of the Bosphorus*)

Plate 11

In an engraving entitled *Troisième vue du Bosphore*, prise à Kandilly," Antoine Melling depicts a kiosk overlooking the Bosporus from a spot well north of Istanbul. This was the type of place to which the wealthy were in the habit of repairing during the heat of the summer to best take advantage of the cooling breezes blowing south from the Black Sea. (Melling, *Voyage pittoresque de Constantinople*, plate 33)

PLATE 12

Even in a landlocked town like Damascus, waterside was considered the ideal place to locate cafés. They were found along the rivers that cut through the town, and similarly in Baghdad, on the Tigris, and in Cairo, on the Nile. The coffeehouse depicted here by William Bartlett seems a bit short on the amenities—patrons sit on mats or carpets on the ground rather than cushioned sofas—yet the clientele is far from humble. Note the hanging lamps: especially in the hotter climates of Syria, Iraq, and Egypt, coffeehouses did particularly good business at night. (John Carne, *Syria, the Holy Land and Asia Minor*)

Plate 13

Although coffeehouses were the preferred places to take coffee from the earliest times, they held no monopoly on the retail sale of coffee. Strolling vendors, such as the one depicted here in an engraving entitled *Vendeur de caffé par les rues* by Jean Baptiste van Moor (1670–1737), were seen on the streets both of the Near East and Europe. Lacking the big charcoal-fueled stove of the coffeehouse, the strolling coffee vendor usually cooked his brew over a small spirit lamp and filled a cup for passers-by. (Le Hay, *Recueil de cent estampes representant differentes nations du Levant* ... [Paris, 1714], plate 56)

PLATE 14

This photograph by the firm of Bonfils captures a strolling coffee vendor in Jerusalem in the 1870s. Here the older *ibrīq* has evolved into the more familiar open-topped pot, while, obviously at the cost of some mobility, the spirit lamp seems to have been replaced with some sort of small, charcoal-burning stove. In the past century, such strolling vendors of coffee (but not of other drinks requiring less elaborate preparation) have virtually disappeared. (Photograph courtesy of the Harvard Semitic Museum © President and Fellows of Harvard College)

Plate 15

This shot of a Cairo coffeehouse by Bonfils shows a somewhat more humble establishment (and clientele) than those depicted earlier. The patrons are seated on a less-than-luxurious bench, and rather than facing the waterfront or an interior fountain, they are practically sitting in the street. This sort of establishment is, and doubtless was, far more common throughout the Near East than the grand coffeehouse, with not just one, but usually several, in every quarter. (Photograph courtesy of the Department of Special Collections, University Research Library, University of California, Los Angeles)

PLATE 16

Denizens seated outside a Turkish coffeehouse, from a stereoptican slide of the late nineteenth century. (B. W. Kilburn Co., 1897. Courtesy of the Keystone-Mast Collection, California Museum of Photography, University of California, Riverside) language agree, and while it is permissible to apply it to other substances by metaphor (*majāz^{an}*), for the purposes of the law, only the exact meaning may be considered.[15]

The other type of argument used in determining what exactly is covered by the prohibition of *khamr* is "custom" (*sunna*), the precedents set by Muḥammad and his companions. These precedents are generally presented in individual "traditions" (*ḥadīth*s), relations of incidents in which Muḥammad or one of his companions said something or acted in a certain way, which are cited to demonstrate the preferred behavior of the believer in a given circumstance.

*Ḥadīth*s concerning drinking and beverages abound. One can be found supporting almost every conceivable position one might take short of claiming *khamr* to be lawful. Of the mass of *ḥadīth*s in the various collections, a few regularly find their way into the arguments in the works of practical jurisprudence. One, after which the position taken by the Shāfi'īs, Mālikīs, and Ḥanbalīs seems most closely modeled, has the prophet saying, "Every intoxicant is prohibited; even a sip [or handful] of [a beverage] of which a *frq* causes intoxication is prohibited."[16] This is clear and to the point, and difficult to circumvent if one admits its authenticity. The Ḥanafīs stopped short of claiming the *ḥadīth* to be spurious, but nonetheless said that it had been abrogated (*mansūkh*) by the later sayings and deeds of Muḥammad. Their interpretation has it that he originally said this to put an immediate stop to flagrant abuses, but later amended it so that a small amount of a drink that was not *khamr* might be allowed.[17] They cite the example of Muḥammad himself drinking something called *nabīdh al-siqāya* after several thirsty circumambulations of the Ka'ba during his final pilgrimage in A.D. 632,[18] and the example of the pious and persistent 'Umar, who is said to have drunk, and ordered others to drink, the definitely alcoholic preparation *muthallath* to aid digestion (*li-istimrā' al-ṭa'ām*).[19]

Another *ḥadīth* attributed to Muḥammad that appears in the arguments of all three schools that opposed alcohol in any form is, "Every intoxicant is *khamr* and every intoxicant is forbidden."[20] Of course, one can take this to mean that, as in the previous case, any quantity of a beverage that intoxicates if taken in large enough quantities is to be considered, at least for the purposes of the law, as *khamr*.

In order to maintain the integrity of their previous arguments, the Ḥanafīs could hardly recognize this redefinition of *khamr*.[21] Their approach to the *ḥadīth* mentioned above, and to a similar one that they prefer ("*Khamr* is prohibited [in and of itself] by its very essence, and the *muskir* of every beverage [is also prohibited]"[22]) is subtly but distinctly different, and based on a nuance of the Arabic language. One may define the Arabic active participle *muskir* either as a substantive, "intoxicant," or as an adjectival participle, "intoxicating," a distinction that makes possible an ingenious bit of legal sophistry. If we take *muskir* to mean "a substance that can make one drunk," that is, an intoxicant, then we cannot avoid the interpretation offered by the Shāfi'īs, Mālikīs, and Ḥanbalīs. If, however, we take it to mean "intoxicating; an amount of a particular beverage sufficient to cause intoxication," then the substance itself is not forbidden, only an overindulgence. This is the interpretation preferred by the Ḥanafīs. Aside from those things that fit into their narrow definition of *khamr*, any beverage, alcoholic or not, is allowed. In this case *muskir* is "the intoxicating [portion]" that "last cup" (*al-ka's al-akhīr*) that pushes one from sobriety into inebriation.[23]

The fact that the Ḥanafīs do not think all alcoholic beverages forbidden does not make their regulations any less strict in other respects. Since they recognize no accidental attribute—namely, that it contains alcohol—that makes a substance *khamr*, those things that *do* fit into their narrow definition of *khamr* cannot be made legal by the removal of that attribute. This position has some curious ramifications. Once uncooked grape juice has been allowed to ferment, it becomes, in its very essence, *khamr*. Boil it, remove the alcohol, and it is still *khamr*, and still forbidden.[24] On the other hand, if you take the grape juice, cook it so that it is reduced by two-thirds, and then allow it to ferment, it is permitted in quantities that will not intoxicate. Clearly, then, by restricting their definition of *khamr*, the Ḥanafīs make it possible for an alcoholic beverage to be legal, while prohibiting one that might have no alcohol at all, simply because *khamr* is not an accidental but an essential attribute, one that no treatment can remove.[25]

Strict as this is, however, it applies only to *khamr* in the narrowest sense. Owing to their acceptance of another *ḥadīth* that also prohibits potent beverages made from dates and raisins, the Ḥanafīs admit these two classes of beverages to the category of *khamr*. Even here, however, they draw a practical distinction between the narrow and broad interpretations of *khamr*, and do not view violation of the latter prohibition as being as serious as violation of the former.

Aside from these, however, the Ḥanafīs recognize no other beverages to be forbidden per se, as long as one does not take such an amount as would make one drunk. In such a case, the fault lies with the drinker, not with the beverage itself. One other admonition they give—and we should bear this in mind when speaking later of the coffeehouse—is that one is allowed to drink "without [the intention of] amusement or wanton diversion" (*min ghayr lahw wa-lā ṭarab*).[26] That is to say, one may drink for refreshment, but without the motive of enjoying the narcotic properties of the draught, or of using it as an accompaniment to unacceptable behavior. Beyond these two reservations, however, Ḥanafī opinion seems generally to follow a broad principle that will be discussed at greater length in the next chapter: "All things are permitted except those things that are [explicitly] prohibited."[27] If a substance does not meet their exacting definition of *khamr*, then it is legal, except in cases of abuse or overindulgence.

By now it should be clear that drunkenness is the key to almost all laws concerning beverages. To the Shāfi'īs, Mālikīs, and Ḥanbalīs, it is the potential of a beverage to make one drunk, if taken in large amounts, that makes it prohibited, and makes the drinker subject to corporal chastisement. To the Ḥanafīs, *khamr* is the only material absolutely and irrefutably forbidden by law, and the only punishable offenses are drinking *khamr* and becoming drunk from any other beverage. Consequently the formulation of a definition of drunkenness is essential to the application of the beverage laws of any of the four schools. As would be expected, the criteria laid down by the various schools differ somewhat. Mālik described the drunk as "one who becomes absent-minded and confused." Shāfi'ī said, "The drunk is one who departs from whatever he has in the way of mild virtue and tranquility [and goes] into [a state of] foolishness and ignorance." Abū Ḥanīfa preferred to see the drunk as "one whose mind leaves him and who knows nothing at all." Ibn Nujaym (d. 1563 [A.H. 970]) expands a bit on this Ḥanafī view of drunkenness, "The drunk who is to be punished is one who comprehends absolutely nothing at all, and who does not know a man from a woman, or the earth from the heavens." Mūllā Khusraw (d. 1480 [A.H. 885]) gives a quasi-medical definition of the phenomenon, "Drunkenness is a state that afflicts a man with the filling of his brain with vapors that rise up into it, so that his reason, which distinguishes between fine things and foul, ceases to function."[28] To the Mālikīs and Shāfi'īs, then, a person who is giddy and boisterous could be considered drunk, and any potion capable of putting one in such a state would be forbidden. According to the Ḥanafīs, one would have to be almost dead-drunk and senseless before he would be considered *sakrān* (drunk), and hence liable to punishment.

COFFEE, "COFFEE EUPHORIA," AND INTOXICATION

Ibn 'Abd al-Ghaffār, in dealing with the question of the possible intoxicating nature of coffee, tells the reader that the problem must be tackled in two stages by: (1) obtaining knowledge of the properties of coffee; and (2) determining what constituted drunkenness.[29] In the light of all that has been said about beverage laws, then, is it possible to maintain that the effects that the coffee drinker experiences could be classified as *sukr*, intoxication?

The immediate temptation is to reply, "Of course not." One finds it rather difficult to imagine how the guidelines established above for intoxication could be applied to coffee. Particularly in the case of Ḥanafī law, it seems next to impossible that one could claim that drinking coffee, in whatever amount, could render one "incapable of distinguishing a man from a woman or the earth from the heavens." Even using the criteria set up by the Shāfi'īs or the Mālikīs, the likelihood of even a gross overindulgence resulting in anything resembling drunkenness is slim indeed.

Unlikely as it seems, however, coffee's possible intoxicating properties were indeed cited as reasons for prohibition. The authors of treatises on coffee devote a great deal of space to a refutation of these claims. Nor can we suspect them of setting up straw men to knock down: they go out of their way to name names. Jazīrī for instance mentions one Shaykh Shams al-Dīn Muḥammad ibn ʿAbd al-Raḥmān al-Qaṭṭān (?) al-Madanī, who likened the intoxicating properties of coffee to those of hashish.[30] The war of words over coffee as an intoxicant must at times have gotten fairly acrimonious. One writer, obviously upset with the tenor of the debate, lodges a countercharge against the opponents of coffee:

> It is not possible for a Muslim to claim that coffee—even in tremendous amounts—inflicts on the drinker the same sort of effects that come from drinking wine or eating hashish or *barsh*:[31] throwing a cover over the intellect, causing changes and metamorphoses in the user to the extent that you could say that he was "drunk".... Whoever claims that drinking coffee puts one in the same state—or even something close—as that of one who drinks or uses these other things is guilty of gross slander.[32]

To claim that coffee was an intoxicant, of course, was to claim that those who drank it—and, as we have seen, this group included many men of prominence in the legal and religious world—were guilty of an offense that carried with it a painful and humiliating corporal punishment. It was an affair not to be taken lightly.

Although these claims were put forward with great seriousness and were the cause of alarm to many, they proved, in point of fact, rather easy to refute. One line of attack, which seems at first a bit odd to the non-Muslim observer but which makes perfect sense in the context of Islamic law, is based on *ijmāʿ*, consensus. A *ḥadīth* attributed to Muḥammad states simply, "My people will never agree on an error." This forms the basis for the theory of *ijmāʿ*, the idea that if the community of the learned in an area on the whole agree on a point of law, it is generally assumed to be valid. It is this weapon that Ibn ʿAbd al-Ghaffār brings to bear on those who claim that coffee is an intoxicant. Coffee, he argues, had been drunk for years, not just anywhere, but in the holiest cities in the Islamic world, by citizens of all sorts, including those of the greatest religious rectitude, without there being the slightest hint of suspicion that it was an intoxicant. It would have been impossible for such a damning characteristic to go unnoticed, and once noticed no one would have allowed the practice to continue even in the basest of spots in the Islamic world, let alone in such august and sublime localities. The fact that it was drunk for years without the slightest suspicion of intoxication, he concludes, demonstrates the approval of the community as a whole, and based on *ijmāʿ*, it simply cannot be an intoxicant.[33]

On the whole, however, the most successful refutations were the same sort of simple observation that one would naturally be inclined to make: the effect of coffee is quite the opposite of that of wine. One author also draws the distinction (perhaps a rather naïve one) between the spirit with which one sets out to drink coffee and that with which one drinks wine:

> If you draw the analogy between coffee and intoxicants you are drawing a false one, since it has been made clear to you how it is quite the opposite in nature and effect. One drinks coffee with the name of the Lord on his lips, and stays awake, while the person who seeks wanton delight in intoxicants disregards the Lord, and gets drunk.[34]

If the sentiment seems a bit lofty, the argument is to the point, and is representative of the general view taken of such claims. As soon as the argument was used, it was refuted with just such evidence based on the obvious: one cannot get drunk on coffee. It seems that the opponents of coffee who resorted to this sort of argument were definitely fighting a rear-guard action.

It was clear to all, of course, that coffee did indeed have an effect on one's mental state. The advocates of coffee not only made no effort to hide this fact, but they quite openly put it forward as one of the best reasons to drink coffee.

Ibn ʿAbd al-Ghaffār gave a capsule summary of what coffee does: "It brings to the drinker a sprightliness of spirit and a sense of mental well-being."[35] Coffee users in the Arabian Peninsula even had their own word, *marqaḥa*, to describe this "coffee euphoria."[36]

Could coffee be outlawed on the basis of this *marqaḥa* itself? The attempt was indeed made. The claim was put forward that any change (*taghyīr* or *taghayyur*) in the physical or mental state of the drinker, even if it did not constitute befuddledness, nonetheless casts doubt on the legality of the potion. Would not even the suspicion of such effects, they asked, tend to make one uneasy concerning the substance?

The advocates of coffee thought this all so much nonsense, and tried to portray it as such:

> If one means by "change" simply the transformation from one state into any other, this is an attack on many things that are clearly licit, such as garlic, onions, leeks, and other spicy foods that have vapors that ascend into the brain. Somebody who eats them will find, after dining, certain changes in himself, such as [illegible] in the body, and signs of redness and protrusion of the eyes. These things are of course apparent to his dining companions, yet none will say anything about these things being forbidden.[37]

Whatever they actually may have thought about the merits of their position, those who claimed coffee intoxicating or, by some other standard, illicitly stimulating, seem to have found themselves retreating on point after point. The sort of argument that they put forward seems to disappear rather early on.

CHAPTER 5

Lethargy, Leprosy, and Melancholia: Coffee and Medieval Medicine

The effects of coffee on the nervous system and the rest of the body are immediately evident to anyone who has ever drunk coffee. Human physiology not having changed much in four hundred years, these effects were noticed by the earliest drinkers as well. As has been mentioned already, it was to attain these effects, notably the "coffee high," *marqaḥa*, that coffee was drunk at all.

It was probably inevitable, then, that the physical consequences of coffee drinking would be cited to call its legality into question. Coffee was demonstrably not intoxicating by the standards of the *sharī'a*. If one could demonstrate, however, that what it did to the mind and body was harmful, it could be attacked and prohibited on those grounds.

The *sharī'a*, of course, recognizes certain classes of foods as forbidden: the prohibition of pork, blood, carrion, and other specific foods, and of the meat of animals not slaughtered according to ritual, is well known. Those foods not specifically mentioned as forbidden, however, are generally assumed to come under the blanket of the principle of "original permissibility" (*al-ibāḥa al-aṣlīya*).[1] In broad terms, what this means is that unless something is expressly prohibited by the Qur'ān or *sunna*, it is permitted. Believers are actively discouraged from letting their piety spill over into sanctimonious asceticism, and from prohibiting those things that God has provided for the believers. The author of the *Iṣṭifā' al-ṣafwa* lodges just this charge against the opponents of coffee, citing the verse:

> Say: "Have you considered the provision God has sent down for you, and you have made some of it unlawful, and some lawful?"
> Say: "Has God given you leave, or do you forge against God?" (Qur'ān 10:59, tr. Arberry)

To consume those things that were clearly prohibited was most certainly a sin, but the proponents of coffee wished to get the idea across that the capricious prohibition of part of God's bounty was a sin as well.[2]

There are exceptional circumstances, of course, where the principle of *al-ibāḥa al-aṣlīya* does not apply. Among these is that, since suicide is forbidden, putting harmful substances into the body is likewise forbidden. In his discussion of hashish, for instance, Ibn al-Jazzār (wrote late sixteenth century) cites this principle:

> [Hashish and similar intoxicants come under the rubric of forbidden materials for a number of reasons], especially [because of] what they bear in the way of harm to the body.... God (His name be exalted) said: "And do not bring about your destruction with your own hand" [Qur'ān 2:195]. What clearer indication can there be of prohibition of the source of destructive things?[3]

It was upon this principle that some of the attempts to suppress coffee were based.

Khā'ir Beg, in the Meccan case of 1511, was among the first to have recourse to this argument concerning coffee.[4] It will be remembered that the muftis whom he had invited to consider the question cited the above-mentioned principle of original permissibility, and said that it could be negated by, among other things, a substance's being harmful to the body. Khā'ir Beg then produced two famous Persian physicians to tell of its harmful nature.[5] This testimony, along with that of those who spontaneously (Jazīrī's account seems to suggest some coaching) rose to tell of the ill effects they had suffered from coffee, convinced the jurists that coffee's harmful nature overruled *al-ibāḥa al-aṣlīya*, and hence could be banned.

Muḥammad ibn Maḥmūd al-Zaynī al-Ḥusaynī, the sixteenth-century author of a short untitled treatise attacking coffee, similarly touches on the theme of the physical harm that can come from coffee drinking.[6] The first part of the work is something of a condemnation of the decline of scholarship, and of medical science in particular. He laments that physicians of his own day had squandered the inheritance of learning left them by the masters of former times, and contented themselves with being considered consummate scholars by the rabble. Thus it was that when coffee began to be used, they paid little attention and made no effort to analyze its nature and decide whether it was harmful. Eventually a young man, identified later in the manuscript as one Beyzāde Muḥammad, went to these quacks seeking relief from his melancholia and lethargy. He got but little satisfaction, and so set out on his own to study the science. He became a physician of the utmost skill, and after much experimentation determined that the growing use of coffee was responsible not only for his own ills, but for those of the general public as well. As a result of his discoveries, he warned against the use of the beverage. The opinion of such a medical man, of course, would itself carry no legal force, but a mufti, acting on these findings, could issue a *fatwā*, and counsel the authorities to prohibit coffee.

The difficulty of grounding any kind of prohibition on such findings is that, as in any other matter where medical science is concerned, opinion is very rarely unanimous.

One could find no better example of this point than the research done on coffee in the late twentieth century. As soon as one group of scientists determines that coffee contributes to a wealth of ills, a separate team releases a report finding nothing harmful at all in the drink. Sixteenth-century medical science faced a similar problem. Those who gave medical arguments for prohibiting coffee were perpetually challenged by others who could produce physicians of eminence to testify that it had positive curative properties. Prohibition built on such supports was in trouble from the start.

There is no need to give a detailed account here of the theoretical basis of medical science among the Arabs as it had been transmitted to and adapted by them from the Greeks, particularly the Greek anatomist and physician, Galen (A.D. 130?–201?). What is important for an understanding of the arguments concerning coffee is that their view of the human body, and the physical world as a whole, was strongly influenced by the theory of the four basic principles and humors as they received it virtually unchanged from Galen.[7] There are four principal humors in the body—yellow bile (*mirra ṣafrā'*), black bile (*mirra sawdā'*), phlegm (*balgham*), and blood (*dam*)—which only in the exceptional case are in perfect equilibrium. In most persons one of these humors predominates, determining his physical nature: bilious (*ṣafrāwī*), melancholic (*sawdāwī*), phlegmatic (*balghamī*), or sanguine (*damī* or *damawī*). Illness can result if the imbalance is too great. Each of these humors, in turn, is linked to two of the four principal "natures" of the physical world—heat, cold, moistness, and dryness. Thus, yellow bile is considered as corresponding to dryness and heat, black bile to dryness and cold, phlegm to moistness and cold, and blood to moistness and heat. Foods, drinks, and medicines are all considered to possess these natures in one degree or another (first degree = a food; second degree = a food or medicine; third degree = a medicine; fourth degree = a poison).[8] If one wishes to treat problems caused by an imbalance of humors, that treatment might include a food or drink comprised of the natures opposite that humor. To treat an overly phlegmatic condition, for instance, which is considered a predominance of cold and moist principles, one would administer a food that is hot and dry. In contrast, a food that is cold and moist was believed merely to aggravate the condition.

Concerning coffee in this scheme of medical theory, the physicians of the time fell into some controversy. Zaynī, being inspired by the researches of his mentor, the aforementioned Beyzāde Muḥammad, to investigate further the "nature of coffee, its harm and benefit, and those herbs and plants that alleviate [its bad effects]," determined that both the husk and the kernel of the coffee bean were cold and dry, and that these natures were to be found in the husk in the highest form of the first degree, and in the kernel in the middle of the second degree.[9] Kâtib Çelebi agreed with this in principle, giving its coldness as a reason why it quenches thirst, and why it "does not burn if poured on a limb, for its heat is a strange heat, with no effect."[10] He goes on to add that the fruit itself is of the third degree of dryness (which would put it firmly in the category of medicaments), but when it is mixed with water this dryness abates somewhat, so that it is only of the second degree of dryness in beverage form. Both these authorities maintain its coldness in direct contradiction to the famed sixteenth-century physician Dā'ūd al-Anṭākī,[11] who tells us that coffee is hot in the first degree and dry in the second. He maintains that claims that coffee is cold are wrong because it is bitter, and all bitter things are hot.[12] He admits, however, that the husks might be hot and the kernels themselves either balanced (*mu'tadil*) or cold in the first degree.[13] Jazīrī, who himself believes coffee to be hot and dry, lays the claim that it is cold and dry on the doorstep of the drink's opponents. They wish, he charges, to draw an analogy between the coldness and dryness of coffee and that of death.[14]

In light of what was said earlier, the significance of these arguments becomes clear. Coffee, if we assume it to be cold and dry, would be expected to aggravate the condition of one in whom the prevailing tendency was toward cold and dryness, that is to say where black bile was the predominating humor. The result of such a condition was generally given to be melancholia. Indeed, this is a common theme running through early texts concerning coffee. It will be remembered that the wretch whose cure eluded the incompetent doctors complained of melancholia and lethargy.[15] In making further investigation, Zaynī determined that by its cold and dry nature coffee did indeed promote melancholia. He added that roasting the beans only served to enhance these properties, and hence their tendency to lead to the disease.[16] Even those authors who do not oppose the use of coffee, or who are actually in favor of it, own that melancholia can be a problem for those with a humoral imbalance.[17] Kâtib Çelebi warns those of a dry temperament, especially those of a melancholic temperament, to avoid large amounts, as this can cause "insomnia and melancholic anxiety."[18] Anṭākī, while avoiding the humoral term *sawdā'*, does nevertheless warn that it might lead to melancholia.[19] These opinions were even picked up and expanded upon by eighteenth-century European writers, such as Louis Lémery.[20] He also remarks that it is not good for those of a bilious temperament, but one does not encounter this remark in any Arabic work except that of Zaynī: "It is strongly suggested that melancholic persons stay away from it, but experience has [also] shown its harmfulness for the bilious."[21] On the other hand, it is considered by its advocates good for those of a warm, moist (sanguine) temperament, and for women,[22] or, if one believes it to be hot and dry, for the cold and moist (phlegmatic) temperament: it dries up moisture, phlegmatic coughs and colds.[23]

In addition to humoral imbalances related to melancholia, physicians ascribed a variety of other ailments to coffee, but these are generally regarded as owing to overindulgence. Among the more prominent of these was insomnia (*sahar*), which is the natural extension of the beneficial property of giving vigor for work at night. It is probably to this reputation of coffee that Francis Bacon refers when he mentions that Turks say that "it excites and disturbs the mind."[24] Coffee was also said to make one lean (*yuhazzilu* or *yuhzilu jidd^{an}*).[25] This was probably due to its reputation for killing the appetite. The desire for food was not the only appetite it supposedly killed: Anṭākī tells us that it "cuts off the desire for sexual activity."[26] This supposed attribute of coffee became well known in Europe, and appears in many contemporary European treatises on the drink.[27]

Anṭākī (along with many European writers who seem to have based their opinions on information from Muslim sources) goes on to list a number of other ills associated with the misuse of coffee. He tells us that it causes hemorrhoids (*bawāsīr*) and recurring headaches.[28] He also adds that one should not take coffee with milk, for fear of contracting leprosy (*baraṣ*). The French writer on coffee and merchant in the Levant, Philippe Sylvestre Dufour (1622–87), adds one other item of cautionary lore, that the Turks regard it as unhealthy to take coffee on an empty stomach, a belief that led to thriving business for the sellers of little biscuits and other foods at the entrances to coffeehouses.[29]

Yet despite these problems, which they associated with the immoderate use of coffee, Muslim physicians were far from unanimous in their condemnation of the drink. Of the physicians whose works we have discussed, Zaynī is alone in his unequivocally hostile attitude toward coffee. After expounding on the evil properties of coffee for the person of melancholic temperament, he proceeds immediately into a treatment of antidotes for the harmful effects of the drink, and gives a list of possible coffee surrogates.[30]

Others, however, suggest many beneficial effects from the use of coffee.[31] Although few medical sources share Anṭākī's opinion that coffee, because it is hot and dry, is beneficial to sufferers of phlegmatic coughs, colds and the like, they do agree with him on several other points. Among these was the recognition of coffee's diuretic effect (*idrār al-bawl*), which presumably was considered good for the kidneys. This benefit is also mentioned by Kâtib Çelebi.[32] Others, however, viewed the diuretic effect of coffee as a danger. The author of the *Iṣṭifā' al-ṣafwa* cites, with obvious contempt, some doctors who claim that through the increased urinary activity:

> The body becomes a mere shadow of its former self; it goes into a decline, and dwindles away. The heart and guts are so weakened that the drinker suffers delusions, and the body receives such a shock that it is as though it were bewitched.[33]

Among the other virtues of coffee enumerated by Anṭākī were that it stops the boiling (or bubbling) of the blood [?] (*wa-yusakkinu ghalyān al-dam*), and prevents smallpox, measles, and bloody skin eruptions.

It is worthy of note that Anṭākī does not list among its beneficial physical effects its stimulating properties. The only place where he alludes to these at all is in his enumeration of harmful effects, listing among these insomnia. Kâtib Çelebi refers to its repelling of sleep (which he attributes to its dryness) without judging the value of this. Jazīrī mentions that this is one of the major benefits of coffee, though the same end could also be achieved by eating little, avoiding tiring activities during the day, and taking a siesta.[34] This, however, cannot properly be considered a physical or medical benefit. It might be good for the soul, since, among other things, it enables one better to perform certain nocturnal devotions,[35] but the physical advantages of this are not stressed by Muslim writers. It is the European writers, who see such stimulating effects as beneficial, who attribute similar opinions to the "Turks."[36]

These European writers also attribute to coffee a number of other physical advantages, which they say the Turks claim, but which one does not find in Muslim sources. Chances are that these are either fabrications, reflections of their own opinions or, more likely, loose and unsubstantiated claims made by nonspecialists, probably overzealous advocates of the drink, whom they may have encountered in coffeehouses and the like. Sir Henry Blount (1602–82), who traveled extensively in the Levant, wrote in the preface of a book on certain digestive problems by one Dr. Rumsey that:

> [The Turks, Arabs, and other Eastern peoples] all acknowledge how it freeth them from crudities, caused by ill dyet, or moist lodging, inasmuch as they, using Cophie morning and evening, have no Consumptions, which ever come of moisture, no Lethargies in aged people, or Rickets in Children; and but few qualmes in women with child; but especially hold it of singular prevention against Stone and Gout. When a Turk falls sick, he fasts and takes Cophie, and if that will not doe, he makes his will, and thinks of no other Physic.[37]

It is conceivable that there might be some claims supportable by contemporary medical theory that it is good for consumption and other problems caused by moisture: this sounds vaguely like what Anṭākī said about phlegmatic conditions. It might also have been thought good for pregnant women: Kâtib Çelebi said that coffee is particularly beneficial for women. Additionally, its purported diuretic effects were probably credited with preventing kidney stones. But nowhere among Muslim writers, even among coffee's staunchest supporters, do we encounter claims for it being a panacea. This we have only from European sources. The benefits to digestion, for instance, I believe are first mentioned in 1609 by the English clergyman, William Biddulph, then subsequently through the 1600s and early 1700s by Francis Bacon, Jean de Thévenot, Audiger, a seventeenth-century French *chef d'office*, and Richard Bradley, professor of botany at Cambridge.[38] How the notion that it had such benefits originally got started, I cannot say, although the idea that hot drinks are good for one's digestive tract seems to have had some currency in seventeenth-century Europe.[39] The point is that on this matter one must approach European sources with a great deal of skepticism, for they seem to have been inclined to pass on whatever anybody said to them about coffee's medicinal value, the more so because so many of them found it unpalatable: they must have ascribed its popularity to its salutary effects, as a sort of oriental health fad.

Medical opinion on coffee as we have it from Muslim sources, then, is at best (or worst) mixed. Not only does it have its advocates and its critics, but even these do not form clear-cut camps. Its critics, like Zaynī, can only substantiate its harmful effects for certain cases, that is, for those of melancholic (and possibly bilious) temperaments. At the same time, its supporters almost always feel constrained to warn that there are those for whom excessive amounts of coffee could be harmful, though they would also argue that the bodily frailties of a few should not dictate the proscription of something to the majority.[40] What is clear, however, is that opinion on coffee was not so unreservedly bad as to warrant a complete suppression running contrary to the doctrine of original permissibility. There were attempts to do this, but they were usually overturned with some speed.

What is worthy of note is that such questions came up at all. It is quite normal that Anṭākī should mention it: he was compiling a list of medical "simples" (*mufradāt*), among which he included the newly introduced "*bunn*." But in the case of Zaynī, who felt coffee deserved a treatise, or of Kâtib Çelebi, who included a chapter on it in his book on the futility of certain kinds of prohibition, it is clear that coffee had become a "question," and only after it became a question was medical attention turned on it. The medical discussion began to search for the evils of coffee only after the decision was made to prohibit it. Nowhere is this clearer than in the Meccan case of 1511.

Most suggestive that the medical arguments were secondary considerations (simply a means to obtain a prohibition that was primarily regarded as desirable for some other reason) is that it was the drink *qahwa*, and not the material *bunn*, that came under attack. The *Risāla fī aḥkām al-qahwa* has a curious passage from which it is clear that medical arguments focused on coffee,[41] although at the time, the chewing of coffee beans was still a fairly routine practice. Jurists actually argued that the beans were legal, but that the drink was not. This, the author of the treatise points out, was all so much rubbish. Whatever harmful effects can be attributed to the drink are present all the more so in the beans, he claims, since at least the water used to prepare *qahwa* helped to temper the properties of the bean. If the drink and not the bean became the target of criticism contrary to prevailing contemporary medical theory, then the reason for such opposition to coffee must indeed be sought elsewhere. Beans could be, and were, consumed everywhere. But coffee was consumed primarily in the coffeehouse.

CHAPTER 6

Taverns without Wine: The Rise of the Coffeehouse

In the sixteenth century, coffee came to enjoy considerable influence on a number of spheres of urban life in the Near East. In the economic sphere, production of and trade in coffee helped breathe life into many areas that only shortly before had been commercially moribund. To the Yemenīs, of course, it was vital, and they took steps (though ones that were, in the long run, futile) to preserve their monopoly. Much of what was grown in the mountains and shipped from the ports of the Yemen had as its ultimate destination the great warehouses of Cairo, where spice and coffee merchants also saw considerable profit. In the seventeenth and eighteenth centuries, Cairene merchants made up for much of what they had lost through European short-circuiting of the Indian spice trade by dealing in coffee.[1] Even if we must regard with suspicion the claim made by the often unreliable Bradley, that coffee was at times used in the marketplaces of Cairo as public tender, it is evident that it was a major commodity for speculation.[2] We know, for instance, that coffee "futures" rose and fell with reports of the varying fortunes of the Red Sea coffee convoys coming from Jidda and Suez. Nor was this economic importance only a consideration of the later centuries. Two Syrians, Ḥakm and Shams, reportedly made a fortune by introducing the habit to the Turks of Istanbul in the mid-sixteenth century.

The single most striking and significant result of the growing use of coffee in the fifteenth and sixteenth centuries, however, was its effect on the social life within the city, town, or village, for around the preparation and sale of this commodity was born a hitherto unknown social institution, the coffeehouse. By the early 1500s coffee's use was no longer restricted to Sufi orders in the Yemen. It had become familiar to and popular among a variety of classes, at least in the Ḥijāz and Egypt. But most significantly, taking it had become a public pastime: the habit struck far deeper roots in the public places intended for that purpose than it did in the home. These public houses where it was served are mentioned immediately and in the closest possible connection with coffee itself, as though an essential part of the definition of coffee is that it is served in these places. In a different context, Ibn ʿAbd al-Ghaffār mentions that although coffee was not as common in Medina as it was in Mecca, in the former it was used at home quite a bit, a fact that he obviously found odd and worthy of note.[3] Writing in the 1600s, Dufour remarks that the Turks seldom took their coffee at home, preferring instead to frequent the coffee shop.[4] This does not mean that coffee was not used much at home; on the contrary, we know that it was, and is, used widely there, and became important in many domestic social rituals. Nonetheless, it seems that, almost from the time that the brewed drink became the standard preparation of *bunn*, the coffee shop became the preferred place to drink it. But, let us first examine for a moment the path coffee took before its consumption in coffeehouses obtained widespread popularity.

COFFEE AND THE SUFI ORDERS

Nothing resembling a coffeehouse appears to have entered into the use of coffee in earliest times by Yemenī Sufis. The taking of coffee in the Sufi *dhikr* was, nonetheless, a social event of a very particular sort. One did not simply toss off a quick cup for a jolt before the *dhikr* and get on with it. To say that coffee came to be considered a sacred drink is overstating the case, but the respect of certain Sufi orders for coffee and its contribution to pious purposes was clearly quite considerable. After all, those who were by tradition credited with the discovery of the drink were often men of no little eminence in Sufi hierology. The Sufis considered it something of a boon, a blessing by use of which they could better execute their devotions. Such a blessing was not to be used lightly or for frivolous purposes. By the early sixteenth century, at the latest, a certain ritual had already come to accompany the distribution and drinking of coffee at the start of the *dhikr*. Ibn ʻAbd al-Ghaffār describes one such ceremony among the Yemenī Sufis at the Azhar:

> They drank it every Monday and Friday eve, putting it in a large vessel (*mājūr*) made of red clay. Their leader ladled it out with a small dipper and gave it to them to drink, passing it to the right, while they recited one of their usual formulas, mostly "lā illāha illā Allāh al-Mālik al-Ḥaqq al-mubīn" (There is no god but God, the Master, the Clear Reality).[5]

The social significance of such a ritual seems to be in the brotherhood of sharing the drink as part of the *dhikr*, of joining together in the action of drinking and religious chant. It is a ritual almost reminiscent of the Christian Eucharist, though certainly without trying to convey the same fundamental theological symbolism.

Nonetheless, while this sort of coffee ceremony is obviously of great social importance, the development of the coffeehouse must be seen as an entirely different phenomenon, involving a quite separate cast of characters. For one thing, the use of coffee is still subsidiary to the *dhikr* as a whole; the *dhikr* is not held for the purpose of drinking coffee, and that act forms a part, but only a part, of the whole ceremony. On the other hand coffee was the raison d'être of the coffeehouse, and remained so, even if with time it was companionship and not the cup which constituted the chief attraction of the place. The pleasure that was the goal of those who went to the coffeehouse tended to come from sources other than religious rapture.

Several intermediary developments were necessary before the rise of shops for the distribution of coffee as centers of social importance. One of these, of course, was that coffee had first to achieve general popularity. Its vogue in Sufi circles was not enough: as long as coffee drinking remained a practice peculiar to a limited group, its effects on the urban milieu as a whole were probably minimal. It may have had a social function important within the small group, but not to the bulk of society. In part, however, the Sufis most likely did contribute to the spread of the popularity of, or at least general knowledge concerning, coffee. This was owing to a fact that has already been mentioned, that Sufis were not on the whole professional men of religion, but people whose livelihood was gotten elsewhere. For religious and certainly social reasons, they belonged to the orders, participated in their worship sessions, and tried in stages to develop their spiritual closeness to the divine, but their day-to-day lives were not confined to the orders. What was perhaps equally important to the broadly based nature of the popularity of coffee, and hence to the development of the coffeehouse as a universal social institution, was that these orders, whatever the actual size of their following may have been, drew their members from a broad spectrum of social groups, so that not merely one stratum of society, but many different strata at once, became aware of the drink.

If the awareness of coffee in society in general in the Yemen and the Ḥijāz can be ascribed to Sufi influences, these cannot fully account for its growing popularity outside the *dhikr*. Indeed, only those with direct access to Sufi *dhikr*s, or in close contact with individual members of the orders, would have had the opportunity to try coffee. Not only have we seen that at times the Sufis rather closely guarded the secrets of their orders, particularly those dealing with stimulants, but also the amount of coffee that they brought out of the Yemen for devotional purposes was probably quite limited. The social use of coffee may be traceable to Sufi practice, but the roots of its social importance must be sought elsewhere.

THE ORIGINS OF THE COFFEEHOUSE

We run into a problem of sources when considering the origins and spread of coffeehouses and the growth of coffeehouse patronage. Useful though Jazīrī's account may be in establishing a date by which coffeehouses were clearly operating in the Ḥijāz and in giving some idea of what they were like, it is of little help in determining where, and in what form, the coffeehouse first developed. The answer to this question is, if anything, more elusive than that of the origins and spread of coffee itself.

From all indications the coffeehouse, like coffee, must be considered an institution of Arab origin. We know that from the end of the sixteenth century the Turks embraced both the drink and the institution with as much, if not more, enthusiasm as their Arab coreligionists. Nonetheless, according to the Ottoman chronicler Ibrāhīm Peçevi

(1574–1650), coffee, the coffeehouse, and all concomitant trappings were introduced as a complete package to Istanbul by the two Syrians Ḥakm and Shams around 1555.[6] It is clear that a discussion of the birth of the institution must begin with the Arab lands.

No concrete evidence has turned up suggesting the existence of an establishment such as the coffeehouse before the beginning of the sixteenth century. The official report of the events in Mecca in 1511 gives the first allusion to the presence of a place for consuming coffee where people gather for social ends as well as refreshment. Khā'ir Beg's chance encounter with the coffee drinkers in the Sacred Mosque led to the disclosure of such places. Their little assembly itself was actually quite primitive, tame and of little interest. They may indeed have been doing as they claimed, following the custom established by earlier Sufis of using coffee during nocturnal devotions, here in celebration of the *mawlid* of the Prophet. Their reluctance to have their activities discovered does, however, suggest something perhaps a bit more sinister. What is of interest to us, however, is that later in the interrogation, when Khā'ir Beg asks about this drink itself, he is told of places "along the lines of taverns" where coffee is served. The account continues with an enumeration of the various forms of revelries purported to go on in such places, many of which were illegal and all of which demonstrated a questionable moral character and intimated a certain sense of impiety.[7] Jazīrī corroborates the existence of such places at that time. In voicing his skepticism concerning the official account and how odd he found it that Khā'ir Beg, as *muḥtasib*, had not heard of coffee, he tells the reader:

> The sale of coffee had taken place quite openly, during the administration of the amir [Khā'ir Beg] and before it, in wine shops (*ḥawānīt*) and coffeehouses that were along the streets and elsewhere; it had also been drunk night and day in the Sacred Mosque.[8]

Jazīrī and other authors actually make it quite clear that there were indeed places for gathering and consuming beverages long before coffeehouses were ever seen—in fact, early accounts generally liken coffeehouses to them. These were, of course, the taverns. That there were taverns, or wine-houses, in late-medieval Near Eastern cities is confirmed in our sources, if only by the frequent accounts of repeated governmental efforts to close them. Actually, what we know of the physical layout, activities, and clientele of the tavern is scanty—perhaps our best sources are the very accounts that deal with coffee, which describe the activities in coffeehouses in terms of those of the tavern.

There is one crucial thing about the tavern of which we can be certain, and this is what makes it entirely unlike the coffeehouse. The tavern was an institution which, by virtue of its being an outlet for a forbidden substance, was always to remain outside the law, or at least condemned to being eternally viewed as morally repellent in the eyes of Muslims. Even if the operation of taverns was tolerated from time to time by the authorities,[9] they were, at least in a Muslim context, invariably connected with low-life activities. The tavern owner occupied roughly the same place on the social scale as the prostitute, the overt homosexual, and the itinerant entertainer.[10] Certainly no Muslim concerned about his reputation would ever risk being seen in such a place, and as such any possible rôle of the tavern as general locus of social activities was presumably limited. The tavern did, however, have a certain social importance to the corps of low-life dregs (and those who, such as bibulous amirs, were above the censure of society) who formed the nucleus of its clientele. But in no way can we assume that the existence of taverns had a profound effect on the patterns of association within urban society as a whole.

If the coffeehouse started as something quite similar in physical amenities and activities to the tavern (and it is clear that by the late-sixteenth century many had reached a scale and grandeur to which taverns could never have hoped to aspire), there was this one vitally important, indeed fundamental, difference: the coffeehouse was a tavern without wine, and as such, in spite of other similarities, it was not a cause of shame to be caught in one. It soon began to draw people from all social strata.[11]

THE SPREAD OF COFFEE AND THE RISE OF THE COFFEEHOUSE

The massive importation of coffee to areas outside the Yemen was most likely undertaken by merchants interested in profit. Sometime after the beverage, or even just its reputation, initially reached an area through the agency of Sufi connections, it must have been realized, by those more concerned with profit than piety, that this might be a lucrative undertaking. They were aware of the warm reception coffee had received in the limited circles into which it had been introduced, and some must have seen the tremendous commercial potential for such a product. But one can imagine that they were faced with something of a marketing problem. Had they merely dumped sacks of coffee in the marketplaces of the larger cities, demand would probably have been very sluggish indeed. Who would buy such a product whose properties, uses, and preparation were a complete mystery to him? Far better to start by selling the already brewed beverage from little stands or shops, in order to build up a demand. As we have seen, this was precisely the course pursued in Istanbul by Ḥakm and Shams. It is likely that most people first tasted coffee in a coffee shop.

The form these new establishments took, their physical arrangement, was in great part determined by that of the already existing places after which they were patterned, or on the actual premises of which they had been built. We thus see three distinct types of coffee outlet emerge early on, which for want of better terms we can label as the coffee stall, the coffee shop, and the coffeehouse. The first, which is for our purposes the least important, is distinguished from the other two in that it is not designed for the on-premises consumption of coffee. It was in essence a "take-out" shop, usually located in a commercial area, for the convenience of those doing business in the markets. It might have been nothing more than a tiny cubicle, where coffee was prepared and then put into the hands of those menials who carried it to the various shops in the market for the refreshment of the merchants and the clients they were cultivating. The custom, as those who have been in markets or offices anywhere in the Near East well know, is still very much alive. It is not at all uncommon to see young men or boys, employees of the coffee stall itself or, more usually, employees of the individual concerns, hustling through the streets and alleys carrying cups and single-serving sized pots on a tray, usually suspended at three points along its circumference by chains or a sort of frame. It is rare for one to be able, even when closing the smallest deal, to avoid having a cup (or more) of coffee or, particularly in Turkey, tea.

Whatever value a cup or two from take-out establishments had for expediting business transactions (and this was, indeed, a social value), it is to the "on-premises" coffee outlets that our attention is turned. These generally fall into two categories determined by size and clientele: the small neighborhood coffee shop, and the larger, "metropolitan" coffeehouse.

Coffee Shops

The first is the small, local shop, which sometimes shared the same function as the aforementioned coffee stalls, acting, among other things, as a "service" café in a quarter, a take-out. There was, in addition, usually some space in the shop for customers to sit and consume their beverage, usually on the high stoop (*maṣṭaba*) that stuck out from the stall, or on a few benches inside the narrow confines of the shop. When the modest confines of the coffee shop were insufficient to accommodate all the customers (particularly on nights when a story-teller was present), patrons spilled out onto the front stoops of shops adjacent and opposite the coffeehouse. These neighborhood coffeehouses seem especially prevalent in Cairo, mentioned by such diverse writers as the Ottoman traveler Evliyā Çelebi (?–1679) and Lane.[12] This type of shop was of course common as well in Syria and Turkey. Biddulph mentions that in Aleppo the patrons sit not so much in the houses, as on the benches near the houses.[13]

Coffeehouses in the Grand Tradition

Far different from these strictly functional shops were the grand-style coffeehouses found in many cities in the Near East. Certainly not all the six-hundred-odd coffeehouses mentioned by D'Ohsson as being found in Istanbul in the time of Selim II (1566–74) were of the grand sort, and perhaps most of them were of the stall type. These small shops exist in Istanbul to the present day.[14] But those coffeehouses that Dufour said were located in the "most important places in town"[15] were apparently quite luxurious. There seems to have been the attempt, especially in Syria and Iraq, to create a park or gardenlike atmosphere, to surround the patron with refreshing sights and sounds unlike those of either the city or the desert: "All the cafés of Damascus are beautiful—lots of fountains, nearby rivers, tree-shaded spots, roses and other flowers; a cool, refreshing and pleasant spot."[16] According to the Portuguese adventurer Pedro Teixeira (1575?–1640), who was in Baghdad at the beginning of the seventeenth century: "[Coffee is] sold in public places built to that end. . . . This house is near the river, over which it has many windows, and two galleries, making it a very pleasant resort."[17] There were grand coffeehouses along major routes in the countryside as well, where the parklike atmosphere is even further in evidence: "In the countryside, they are shaded by great trees and trellises of vines, with large benches on the outside."[18] Of course, even the large, enclosed type of Istanbul coffeehouse furnished the opportunity for al fresco enjoyment for those who so wished: "Outside the building as well there are benches of masonry, with mats on them, where they can sit who wish to be out in the open air and watch the passers-by."[19] Quite often there would be great lamps placed along the ceilings of the coffeehouses, because of their popularity at night, particularly at two times of the year: in summer, when the cool of the evening would draw people out; and in Ramaḍān, when many would choose to break their fasts with a cup or two, and when there were the most frequent performances by story-tellers.

COFFEE PREPARATION AT THE COFFEEHOUSE

Whatever the differences between the neighborhood coffee shops and the metropolitan coffeehouses may have been, they both possessed certain common physical characteristics. Most, even the largest, consisted of one large main room, which served both as kitchen and salon for the patrons. In modern times the latter is set up with tables in the familiar "restaurant" arrangement, but formerly the customers sat on long benches or divans stretching along the walls. In some corner of this main room was the heart of the establishment, the "service bar" where coffee was prepared and picked up by waiters. While on the whole there were certain standard procedures for preparing coffee, there were enough variations in practice to warrant a short discussion of how the drink was actually prepared, and what variations there were in materials used, apparatus, and cooking methods.

Materials

In preparing coffee, three basic sorts of materials were involved: water, ground coffee, and additives. Of the first there is little to say. None of the sources makes any mention of special considerations concerning the water used. The question of additives is also one that gets only cursory treatment. From all accounts, sugar was seldom if ever used, while milk was almost never added.[20] Occasional use was made in former times, as it is in some places today, of cardamom, and there are reports of mastic or even ambergris being added.[21] The majority of the recipes and descriptions, however, list as the only ingredients coffee and water. Other, less wholesome but more stimulating additives were often employed, but these will be discussed in the next chapter.

A rather more thorny problem is involved in trying to determine exactly what sort of coffee was used to make the usual brew. In his initial definition of *qahwa*, Jazīrī tells us that it is made from either the husks of the bean alone, or from the husks and the kernel of the bean.[22] In another place, he mentions a legal question put forward requesting a *fatwa*: "What do you say concerning coffee, prepared from the *bunn* and its husks? A description of it is that a certain amount of *bunn*, or its husks, is taken and boiled in water."[23] It has already been noted that Bradley reports that in the summer the Arabs use the husks, and in the winter the kernels of the bean, to benefit from the application of the "cold" nature of the husks in the summer, and the "hot" nature of the kernels in the winter.

Some descriptions refer almost exclusively to using the husks. The description initially given Khā'ir Beg of coffee, that it is "cooked from the husks of the seed called *bunn* that comes from the Yemen," is one example. The Jesuits Paez and Monserrat, traveling in the Yemen in 1590, were given coffee, which was "water boiled with the rind of the fruit which they call Bune,"[24] and La Roque tells us that "people of quality" in the Yemen made coffee solely from the husks, producing a pleasant beverage.[25] Lane suggests that this was probably a regional habit of the peninsula,[26] and the evidence would bear this out. Niebuhr, who traveled extensively in Turkey, Egypt, and Arabia (and who was accompanied by the Swedish botanist Peter Forskål [1736?–63] until the latter's death), draws a sharp differentiation between the two types of drink:

> It is odd enough that, in Yemen, the proper country of which the coffee plant is a native, there should be so little coffee drunk. It is there called *Bunn*, and is supposed to have heating effects upon the blood. The favorite drink of the Arabians of this province is prepared from the husks of coffee-beans, slightly roasted, and pounded. It is called *Kahwe*, or more commonly *Kisher*. It tastes like tea, and is thought refreshing.[27]

From this we not only have corroboration of the existence of the distinct categories *qahwa bunnīya* (coffee made from kernels or whole beans) and *qahwa qishrīya* (coffee made exclusively from the husks) mentioned by Jazīrī, but also evidence of the differences in local tastes between what Niebuhr saw in his earlier travels in the Levant and what he encountered in the Yemen. Our other European sources generally talk of the "grain" or "seed" being used, but these terms are too vague for any clear information to be derived from them. Biddulph, however, tells us that coffee was "made from a kind of Pulse like Pease,"[28] a clear indication that it was the center, and not the husk, of the berry that was used. All indications are that except in the Yemen, and possibly for a while in the Ḥijāz, the kernel of the bean was the primary source for the ground coffee used to make the drink. It is worthy of note, however, that *qahwa qishrīya* is still widely used in the Yemen, and is indeed quite similar in taste and appearance to what Niebuhr describes. The best way to describe it would be that it looks and tastes like a sort of oddly spiced tea.

Apparatus

Concerning whether coffee was powdered through use of a mortar and pestle or ground in a mill, evidence suggests that both were used. Lane, for instance, speaks in two places of coffee being "pounded" after it was roasted, a term that suggests the former treatment.[29] Nonetheless, other sources make it clear that they are referring to a milling process.[30] The Flemish traveler Joannes Cotovicus (d. 1629) even speaks of coffee being ground "with the use of a hand-mill" (*molā trusatili*) or by a grinding stone.[31] The crushing apparatus used may be of little significance to the physical plan of the coffeehouse in any event, since, at least in the later centuries, it seems that there were separate coffee millers who supplied the coffee shops with all the coffee they needed.[32]

Thévenot's report of there being large caldrons in which coffee is cooked in the coffeehouses might strike the reader as a bit odd, since now it is almost always prepared freshly for each customer, or at least in relatively small batches, which in a busy establishment are used up in a matter of minutes.[33] Coffee generally will not tolerate being kept warm without seriously deteriorating, and such is especially true of Middle Eastern coffee. There is, however, corroborative evidence from Jazīrī that at times coffee was prepared, or at least stored, in large vessels: a large clay pot (*mājūr*) of it was seen at the Sufi meeting at the Azhar;

Khā'ir Beg had it brought into the council of muftis in a sort of tub or vat (*mirkan*).[34] It is conceivable that, used quickly enough, coffee made in such large amounts would not suffer significant deterioration. More often, however, the cooking vessels used seem to be of the smaller type, more akin to those still used. Dufour's description of a seventeenth-century coffee pot is typical:

> In the Levant, for cooking coffee they use a type of kettle made of copper, tinned inside and out, of a rather particular design, which has still not been duplicated in France. They call it an *ibriq*.... I've found it quite suitable for this purpose, since the base, which is broad, receives more of the flame, in consequence of which the water boils more quickly. Additionally, the opening is quite narrow, to better retain the volatile essence of the brew.[35]

The smaller size of such pots is indicated by the reports that coffee is usually poured into serving cups immediately after cooking. Nonetheless, we must consider it a possibility that in these coffee shops there were large caldrons kept hot from which individual cups of coffee were drawn.

The serving cups themselves were, from even the earliest accounts, invariably of either clay or porcelain, depending on the wealth of the establishment and its clientele. The German physician and botanist Leonhard Rauwolff (d. 1596) tells us of coffee being drunk from "deep little dishes of earthenware or porcelain."[36] Jazīrī is particularly keen to make a point of this, for he wished to draw a clear distinction between coffee cups, which were "bowls of clay" or, in Jidda, porcelain, and the wine cup (*ka's*), which was often glass (*billawr*).[37]

Methods

The procedure for preparing coffee seems to have changed little over the centuries, from the descriptions given by Jazīrī. One deviation from standard practice mentioned is that after cooking, the pot is set aside and the coffee allowed to settle and cool.[38] This practice was, and is, more particular to the coffee drunk in the Arabian peninsula, true "Arab" coffee, which is still prepared in covered pots of a rather different design from those used in the Levant. It is cooked, the sediment allowed to settle, and then the clear liquid is decanted into another pot, into which fresh coffee is added, and is cooked again. This process may be repeated several times, resulting in an intense brew, served free of sediment, in tiny cups, far smaller than the usual "Turkish" cup. Most other accounts, however, allude to what we would call "Turkish" coffee, speaking of the necessity of swift decanting, sediment and all, into cups and serving. Thévenot supplies a good account of standard preparation:

> When they wish to drink coffee, they take a specially made kettle called an *ibrik*, and having filled it with water put it on to boil. When it does so they add the powdered coffee, using about a healthy spoonful for every three cups of water. When this boils again, one must pull the pot quickly off the fire, otherwise it will boil over, since it rises very swiftly in the pot. When one has thus allowed it to boil ten or twelve times it is poured into porcelain cups."[39]

THE SUCCESS OF THE COFFEEHOUSE

It may seem to those who have traveled in the Near East that, in making the assumption that the coffeehouse sprang logically from the commercial need to sell the prepared beverage, we are overlooking another obvious possibility. One still finds in Istanbul and the cities of the Levant street vendors who sell everything from kebabs and grilled fish to *vişne* (sour cherry juice) and even water. Why was this type of sale not applied to coffee as well?

Coffee, quite simply, has to be prepared and consumed in a particular manner, one that precludes a completely mobile operation. Coffee, particularly in the form in which it was and is drunk in the Near East, must be served and drunk hot. European accounts emphasize that Arabs and Turks liked their brew scalding, "as hot as they could suffer it."[40] If coffee is to be served at such a temperature, a strolling coffee vendor would not be able merely to prepare it in large quantities ahead of time and carry it around, selling it as he went, without some sort of elaborate apparatus for keeping it warm.

Similarly, the customer cannot merely have a steaming cup of coffee shoved into his hands and be expected just to swallow it down. Even assuming he were sufficiently impervious to pain to deal in such a manner with a drink "as close to boiling as possible," he would find the experience far from pleasant. Turkish coffee, when first poured, is turbid with *telve*, the powdery grounds which, left undisturbed, settle in about a minute into a thick mud at the bottom of the cup, leaving an inch and a half or so of clear coffee on top. This may very well be what accounts for the fact that the Turks do not generally toss their coffee down in a couple of gulps, but sip it more slowly.[41] All this is best accomplished with a stationary and relatively protected place of consumption. Coffee demands that you take your time.

This consideration must not, however, be overstated as contributing directly to the general physical attributes of the coffeehouse. There were indeed exceptions to the general principle of stationary sale, cases where such a hot beverage was distributed. Lane tells us of coffee being passed out to people in the street by servants during a circumcision procession in nineteenth-century Cairo,[42] although this was quite obviously a small-scale undertaking, performed more to satisfy custom than to attract it. Of more immediate significance to us, there were indeed strolling coffee sellers—this was, in fact, the way many "Levantine" coffee cooks in seventeenth-century Paris peddled their wares. It should, however, be pointed out that even these peddled their brew from door-to-door—they cooked it over a little spirit stove, and filled the customer's cup at his door.[43] We have some references to coffee sellers in Europe or the Near East who actually sold it to passers-by in the streets, and photographic evidence from the nineteenth century testifies to their existence even then. Yet they, like their brethren who peddled it from door-to-door, have subsequently disappeared.

If we grant that the tavern provided the most convenient model for those wishing to introduce coffee to the public at large, why then would people continue to frequent such shops once they became familiar with the methods of preparation? In the Near Eastern context we are speaking of a society without any significant restaurant culture. The inhabitants of the sixteenth-century Muslim city were, even by the standards of their contemporaries from Europe, short on dining spots. George Sandys bemoaned the lack of such places in "inhospitall Turkie."[44] Eating outside the home was, and in some places remains, a habit alien to most.

The answer is not to be found solely in relation to the drink itself. It is, of course, likely that the proprietors of the coffeehouses successfully created the demand for a kind of taste which they, with their arcane skills, were best prepared to duplicate. Yet it is not primarily in this that we must look for the answer, but rather in the fact that the coffeehouse provided the sixteenth-century urbanite with an excuse to do something that he obviously had a desperate urge to do—to get out of the house. We seem to have a situation where there was an underlying and previously dormant social itch, and the coffeehouse at least provided a means, and more importantly one that was not altogether disgraceful, for giving it a bit of a scratch. One went to the coffeehouse not merely because one wished to drink coffee. One went to the coffeehouse because one wished to go out, to spend the evening in the society of his fellows, to be entertained, to see and be seen. There is no more eloquent testimony to this than the relative success enjoyed by the coffeehouses over the door-to-door coffee seller, and the ultimate disappearance of the latter.

The coffeehouse, introduced, as it seems, out of mercantile motives, given its general shape by imitation of taverns and considerations determined by its method of preparation, thrived because it catered, perhaps initially by accident, to a real social need. The very fact that it offered something different, something which was indeed, as its critics claimed, *bid'a*, innovation, allowed it to take its place without disturbing already established patterns of life. As has been mentioned, it was in some way part of the proper life of a decent person to take his meals at home. If it had even occurred to somebody to establish such places, aside from those for itinerant outsiders in the *khāns*, where one went to have meals, it would have seemed very odd indeed. But the coffeehouse in no way disrupted this aspect of life. Rather, it offered something extra, outside previous experience, and as such could be fit into one's routine.

Physical comforts of a tremendous variety were offered the patron of the coffeehouse. In the summer, particularly in the warmer climates, the cool shade trees, the splashing of rivers or fountains, and the general parklike atmosphere doubtless provided a refreshing contrast to the heat, noise, dirt, and smell of the streets. Even the indoor coffeehouse, at least if it was of the better sort, probably had fountains and soft cushions for the patrons, and the sense of physical and spiritual well-being imparted by both atmosphere and caffeine must have held a powerful attraction for potential customers.

Inviting though all these sensual delights were, in the long run what kept the coffeehouse jammed was the fact that its facilities for sitting and having a cup offered the perfect setting for consorting with one's fellow patrons. This rôle of the coffeehouse as locus of social intercourse was clearly what, in the end, fueled the controversy surrounding coffee. The moral question had nothing to do with what one drank in the coffeehouse. Once we learn not to be diverted by the scent of this red herring, the real questions and social anxieties emerge, those concerning why one came, with whom one associated, and what one did alone or in groups in these places.

CHAPTER 7

Society and the Social Life of the Coffeehouse

The fuss over individual and collective activities in the coffeehouse allows us to take in two levels of society at once. On the surface, we have a glimpse of coffeehouse society proper. Our attention is directed toward what went on and why, how the patrons amused themselves and were amused by others, and who associated with whom. What is, in addition, unintentionally revealed is an image of society as a whole, of how those who participated in the dispute over coffee viewed both the ideal and real rôle of man in his community and the world. When a society (or those who claim to be the moral spokesmen of that society) perceives something as objectionable, it tells us almost as much about itself as it does about the object of its displeasure. We can learn much of its expectations, its norms, and its social values. If we can get some idea of just what values were thought to be jeopardized by the coffeehouse, it is then possible to determine what aspects of urban social life the ultimate success of the coffeehouse affected, and how some of those things that were initially the very targets of criticism came in time to be accepted norms: how, in short, the society may have been in some small way forever changed by the new institution.

PATRONS

Our sources have much to say concerning who exactly went to the coffeehouse, but on some points they are mutually contradictory. Lane, discussing the coffeehouses of Cairo in the nineteenth century, was of the opinion that those who frequented the places were almost exclusively from "the lower orders." Alexander Russell makes a similar observation concerning Aleppo in the eighteenth century, dismissing those he saw in the places as "vulgar." Other authors, however, are almost unanimous in portraying coffeehouses as magnets for a much broader spectrum of society. Kâtib Çelebi depicts the behavior of the clientele as far from refined, but nonetheless includes in their number customers from almost every segment of society: "... the people [who went to coffeehouses], from prince to beggar, amused themselves with knifing one another." Dufour, writing about Istanbul, says that all but the "very high" come to the coffeehouse, and D'Ohsson, making a similar exception concerning his eighteenth-century contemporaries, includes among those who flocked to the newly opened coffeehouses in sixteenth-century Istanbul "beys, nobles, officers, teachers, judges and other people of the law."[1] The Venetian bailo, Gianfrancesco Morosini, paints a vivid picture of the coffeehouse patron in 1585:

> All these people are quite base, of low costume and very little industry, such that for the most part they spend their time sunk in idleness. Thus they continually sit about, and for entertainment they are in the habit of drinking, in public, in shops and in the streets—a black liquid, boiling [as hot] as they can stand it, which is extracted from a seed they call Caveè ..., and is said to have the property of keeping a man awake.[2]

Pedro Teixeira reports that in Baghdad "[coffee] is prepared and sold in public houses built to that end; wherein all men who desire it meet to drink it, be they great or mean."[3] Thévenot is particularly emphatic about the universal appeal of the coffeehouse: "All sorts of people come to these places, without distinction of religion or social position; there is not the slightest bit of shame in entering such a place, and many go there simply to chat with one another."[4] Of course, local custom might have been involved in determining who came to a coffeehouse. Also possible is that by the time Russell and Lane wrote, much of the novelty of the places had worn off in the eyes of the local "beautiful people," leaving it to the less well-to-do as a source of cheap amusement.

From the assumption that all classes went to coffeehouses it does not of necessity follow that all classes went to the same coffeehouse, or that the coffeehouse was in any way a place where social betters and inferiors mingled, where urbanites from different quarters associated. The degree to which these social barriers were broken down was most likely determined by the location and type of establishment about which we are speaking. Niebuhr mentions some odd, innlike establishments that dotted the Yemeni countryside; with these we need not concern ourselves. They were intended strictly for the itinerant trade, and probably had little to do with the social lives of the locals.[5] On the social rôle of the coffee shop in the villages, there is again little to be said, not because it was not important in the context of the village, but because village life is so infrequently discussed in the mostly urban-oriented historical sources.

Within the main object of our interest, the urban centers, we may assume that the small neighborhood coffee shop was operated exclusively for local traffic, in most cases catering to a relatively homogeneous clientele. The same may obviously be said for the "take-out" coffee stall, which was an integral part of market complexes, and in later times included as part of the general plan for newly endowed market areas.[6] Such places provided the coffee that doubtless accompanied social activities elsewhere, but were not themselves centers of such activity. The larger, more elaborate coffeehouse obviously was of greater potential as such a place of mingling. Some were situated to serve a particular clientele, such as those near the citadel of Cairo, which got much business from the garrison.[7] Others were in areas of great commercial activity, such as the chaotic Tahtakale neighborhood, the site of the first coffeehouses in Istanbul. In Damascus, there were several large coffeehouses which, judging from their scale and location at the hub of city life, were clearly intended to draw in all those who for any reason were in the central part of the town. One near the Sinānīye mosque, of particularly large dimensions, was simply called "the Grand Café"; near the gate of the citadel was another, with a river passing along one side, and shade trees.[8] If the majority of the thousands of urban coffee shops were of the humble sort, we still must assume that the larger ones in the central portions of the city were intended to attract customers from every quarter who were in that area.[9] One can presume that mixing in such places was not only across quarter lines, but across class lines as well. Even smaller cafés, which appeared in clusters at particularly important crossroads or along popular promenades, might also have served such an end.[10]

Thévenot, however, is probably a bit too sanguine in assuming the coffeehouses to be centers of interconfessional commingling. In Islamic society, the general tolerance for the protected Christian and Jewish minorities came accompanied with the understanding that the minorities were to remain both separate and unequal. The *sharī'a* sets out certain formal disadvantages for the minority communities, erecting clear legal barriers between the believer and the unbeliever that can be breeched by no means except conversion. These walls were made all the more impenetrable by the all-too-human tendency toward contempt for those outside one's own group. These barriers were exceedingly formidable, and it is highly unlikely that they would break down over a cup, a pipe, and a relaxing game of chess. It is not even certain that any single coffeehouse catered to an ecumenical clientele. One may doubt that any given group would be formally barred, but in a society where the informal rules made it quite clear who belonged where, formalized segregation would be unnecessary. If you did not belong, you would not be comfortable.

In this one respect, at least, the tavern probably had a more heterogeneous clientele than the coffeehouse. The former was perforce run exclusively by non-Muslims, ostensibly for non-Muslims (to serve wine to a Muslim, or even to flaunt this loathsome habit in the sight of Muslims, was in some cases a capital offense). Some Muslims, however, doubtless came to the tavern, and these social misfits must have regularly had to rub shoulders with their confessional inferiors.

The coffeehouse, on the other hand, was essentially a Muslim establishment, in spite of all the conflict and controversy surrounding it. This controversy arose, indeed, because the coffeehouse *was* a particularly Muslim institution, not just some dive developed by and for the protected unbelievers. Connected in its embryonic stages to religious worship (albeit at times of questionable orthodoxy), nurtured, in both pious and unabashedly secular forms, in the holy and exclusively Muslim precincts of the Ḥijāz, and later introduced into Cairo through the portals of the Azhar, the coffeehouse was, in birth and development, a very Muslim institution. It may have indeed been *bid'a*, innovation, but if so, it was one springing from the native soil, indeed the sacred heartland, of Islam, not one introduced from the lands of the unbelievers.[11] Except in those times when it was entirely forbidden by civil authorities, coffee trade was solely the domain of Muslims. They, of course, dominated the caravans or convoys that plied, respectively, the Ḥijāz and the Red Sea. In addition, wholesale trade in coffee was, at least in Cairo, exclusively in their hands.[12] Opening or operating a coffeehouse did not of necessity detract from one's good name in the eyes of the pious, nor did it seem contradictory to one's functions as a member of the religio-legal elite. Some ulema in Cairo, even as early as the late sixteenth century, amassed considerable personal fortunes in coffee speculation; and in the eighteenth century, one can cite the example of at least one professor at the Azhar who owned, among other properties, a coffeehouse.[13] The Egyptian chronicler Isḥāqī (wrote 1623) tells of Ahmet Paşa, governor of Egypt in the late sixteenth century, increasing his prestige among the ulema and poor by funding, among other public works, coffeehouses in Būlāq and the Rashīd quarter.[14] Nor was patronage of a coffeehouse restricted to those whose sole concern was necessarily this world and not the next. Various religious functionaries (particularly men of a relatively high degree of religious learning, as opposed to minor mosque functionaries, a consideration we shall get back to) did not scruple to be seen in the coffeehouses of Istanbul. Moreover, in addition to the other entertainments that we shall discuss further on, there are occasional reports of there being those with some religious content. Niebuhr not only tells of "Mullachs, or poor scholars" entertaining customers with orations and stories, but on at least one occasion, in Aleppo, he saw a man of some wealth and learning who took it upon himself to go around to coffeehouses delivering harangues for the spiritual improvement of the customers.[15]

All this is not to suggest that Christians and Jews did not frequent coffeehouses. On the contrary, if only from the fact that Greeks and Armenians are constantly cited as having done much to introduce coffee drinking to Europe, we know that they were quite familiar with it.[16] But would they have been regular habitués of a coffeehouse with a predominantly Muslim clientele? It is, at best, unlikely. Coffee and the coffeehouse had developed very strong ties to the greater part of Muslim society. It was not necessarily considered a shameful business, work fit only for *dhimmīs*, to be involved in trafficking in coffee, either on a wholesale or retail level. In addition, the coffeehouse became curiously bound, if only indirectly, to the daily ebb and flow of the religious life of the Muslim community: its particular popularity on nights of Ramaḍān suggests its gradual inclusion in the set of socio-religious habits connected with that season when religious duties regulated the pace of life. In brief, Muslim society had taken it as its own institution, one in which the participation of non-Muslims was not essential and in which, in certain circumstances, their presence might be considered offensive. We must assume that the general tendency in the society toward religious separation applied to the coffeehouse as well.

ACTIVITIES AND ENTERTAINMENTS

Ibrāhīm Peçevi, in his chapter on the introduction of coffee to Istanbul, tells of how those who would formerly have spent large sums giving dinners at home for their friends could, with the coming of the coffeehouse, entertain for only a few coins.[17] The novelty of such activity was obviously quite striking in the sixteenth and seventeenth centuries, and there is an implied revolution in the way people perceived of how things were to be done. The proffering of hospitality was no longer something that could be undertaken solely in one's home. No longer was a host necessarily surrounded by possessions, wife, children, slaves, and all the trappings and symbols of proprietorship that had always been present when one was extending to the guest the full resources of his household. The act of hospitality could now be transferred to a public place where one's responsibilities, and perhaps prestige, as host were more limited. This would imply a subtle shift in the relationship of host and guest, and a break, if only symbolic, with old values. There, in the coffeehouse, one could play host for relatively little outlay, and the "sport" seeking a reputation for magnanimity could, for a trifling sum, even show his generosity to those who were not originally members of his party:

> When someone is in a coffeehouse, and he sees people whom he knows come in, if he is in the least ways civil, he will tell the proprietor not to take any money from them. All this is done by a single word, for when they are served with their coffee, he merely cries "giaba" [Turkish: *caba*], that is to say, "Gratis!"[18]

Such substitute hospitality must have seemed, to some, a rather sham and ridiculous way for the tightwad to flaunt his generosity. An Ottoman visitor to Cairo at the end of the sixteenth century wrote:

> When *jundis* [soldiers] go, for instance, in a coffeehouse and there have to get change for a gold coin, they will definitely spend it all. They regard it as improper to put the change in their pocket and leave. In other words, this is their manner of showing their grandiosity to the common people. But their grand patronage consists of treating each other to a cup of coffee, of impressing their friends with one [cup] of something four cups of which costs one *para*.[19]

Whether the advent of the coffeehouse meant the demise of the dinner party or not, it certainly does seem, in this period, to have become something of the center of such social contact among males as had to do with neither business nor religion.[20] Later we shall explore more deeply the long-term social implications of this fact, but here it is appropriate first to describe the nature and quality of social activities in the coffeehouse.

Conversation

Aside from the more formal pastimes and diversions that will be discussed below, the coffeehouse was above all a place for talk: serious or trivial, high-minded or base, that place more than any other seemed to lend itself to the art of conversation. Amid the relaxing surroundings and atmosphere of leisure afforded by the grand metropolitan coffeehouse, caffeine-stimulated talk thrived, perhaps even more than it did on the mats and carpets of the mosque. Quite often the talk was of the light, frivolous kind, the work of the coffeehouse wit hauling out the often-told tale for the consumption of new listeners. Dufour tells us that men would divert themselves with vague conversations "about nothing in particular, or with humorous tales." The Elizabethan clergyman, William Biddulph, reports mainly "idle and Alehouse talke" in the coffeehouses of Aleppo.[21] Such harmless banter was probably not, on the whole, considered particularly impious. Some of those more rigid in their views of how people ought to spend their time, however, did find in such activities the suggestion of a certain laxity of moral character. Among them, paradoxically, was Jazīrī, who complains of the seriousness of the *dhikr* being replaced in the practice of coffee drinking by jests and the telling of tall tales.[22] The expression of this opinion, however, may have been intended to emphasize the pious applications of the drink and to combat the arguments of those who opposed coffee altogether.

The loose banter of the coffeehouse was sometimes viewed as far from harmless. The patrons of the coffeehouse, it seems, were not immune to the temptation often to disregard the strict letter of the truth when relating stories about others, particularly about women. A writer who was otherwise favorably disposed to coffee was particularly indignant about this aspect of coffeehouse life:

> [Among the abominable practices in coffeehouses is that patrons] will really extend themselves in slander, defamation, and throwing doubt on the reputations of virtuous women. What they come up with are generally the most frightful fabrications, things without a grain of truth in them.[23]

Making false accusations (*qadhf*) about the sexual propriety of a chaste woman (*muḥṣan*) is indeed contrary to the *sharī'a*: it is a corporal offense, punishable with eighty lashes.[24] Otherwise, the habit of telling tales about others is not punishable, but is regarded as distasteful in the extreme.

Coffeehouse conversation was not entirely jejune. Peçevi describes the often intense literary activity among the patrons.[25] As was to happen later in Europe, the coffeehouse became something of a literary forum; poets and writers would submit their latest compositions for the assessment of a critical public. In other corners of the coffeehouse, there might be heated discussions on art, the sciences or literature.[26] Again, there would seem little in such activity to provoke censure, although the secular, worldly subject matter might in itself be enough to leave the participants open to attack.

The introduction of certain other topics for discussion was inevitably to lead to direct attacks from the politically powerful. Public affairs furnished much of the fuel for comment and criticism among coffeehouse patrons.[27] In place of newspapers or public forums, the coffeehouse quickly became the place of exchange of information, where news of the palace or Porte was spread by word of mouth. Perhaps, in those places where men of some position were to be found, the ancient and revered institution of the news "leak" was not unknown. One wishing to hear the latest news—or, more likely, the freshest rumors—needed only to station himself in the coffeehouse for a short time. "Young idlers," says D'Ohsson, "spend whole hours in them, smoking, playing draughts or chess and discussing affairs of the day."[28]

A forum for the public ventilation of news, views, and grievances concerning the state possessed the potential for becoming a political "clubhouse" from which concerted action might be taken by those with a common distaste for the regime. As such, it could not help but appear a bit suspicious to those in authority. In fact, there is much to suggest that often the patrons were not merely proponents of free speech, but were more the type for whom words alone would not suffice. More than one coup d'état has been launched from, or at least plotted in, a coffeehouse. D'Ohsson attributes the most energetic and complete closing of coffeehouses in Istanbul to just such a problem. By the time of the sultanate of Murat IV (1623–40), coffeehouses had become "meeting places of the people, and of mutinous soldiers."[29] Murat was neither the sort of man to risk the same fate Osman II (r. 1618–22) had suffered a decade earlier, nor the sort of man to take half-measures when he chose to deal with a problem.[30] In 1633, on the pretext of preventing the disastrous fires that sometimes got started in coffeehouses, he ordered them torn down, and coffee, as well as tobacco and opium, banned. Several decades later, coffeehouses in Istanbul were still closed, "desolate as the heart of the ignorant," though they were to reopen in the last quarter of the century.[31]

In dealing with the problem of sedition in the coffeehouse, not all governments employed such heavy-handed methods. With a bit of applied creativity some even found that they could turn the situation to their own advantage. In the nineteenth century, Muḥammad ʻAlī's government had a rather sophisticated way of dealing with factious elements in Cairene coffeehouses. Realizing that such public forums for loose talk could easily be exploited, police spies were often planted in coffeehouses to gather information to which the government otherwise might not have been privy until the mischief of the seditious had been effected.[32]

Gaming

As early as the Meccan incident reported by Jazīrī, games, as well as talk, were a vital part of coffeehouse life: "People gather in the places where [coffee] is sold and play chess and *manqala* and other [games] for stakes."[33] It is hardly surprising that such diversions were seen in the earliest coffeehouses, since it would seem that they were among features adopted from the tavern.[34] Chess became quite popular in the coffeehouses in Turkey.[35] Backgammon (*nard*), which was already known, must have quickly become a favorite: it is perhaps to this that D'Ohsson refers when he speaks of the Turks playing "draughts," although we cannot rule out the possibility of some other game. It is unclear whether card games, so often seen in the modern coffeehouse, were in use in early times. They are not mentioned in early sources, and it is possible that they were introduced later from Europe, although some evidence exists for their use in this and earlier centuries.[36]

There is some doubt as well concerning the prevalence of gambling connected with these games. On one level, there is no mention of hard-core dicing games. Chess, however, was played at times for stakes,[37] and Jazīrī's description, or rather that of the official report concerning the 1511 incident in Mecca, would lead one to believe that gambling was something of the rule in coffeehouses in the

Ḥijāz in the sixteenth century. Sandys, on the other hand, was of the opposite opinion concerning Istanbul:

> Of Cards and Dice they are happily ignorant; but at Chesse they will play all the day long: a sport that agreeth well with their sedentarie vacancie, wherein not withstanding they avoid the dishonest hazard of money.[38]

Other sources that mention games have little to say either way on the subject, although Russell flatly states that he saw little if any gambling involved in the games played by Arabs and Turks at Aleppo in the eighteenth century.[39]

Gambling of any description, of course, would be enough to bring the moral character of the place where it was practiced into question. Even if there was no gambling involved in these games, however, that fact alone would not be sufficient to remove all taint of impropriety and loose morals from the players or the place that would allow such activity. There is, quite simply, some question of the legal status of games such as chess, even if no betting takes place. The taint on backgammon is, if anything, worse.[40] It is, in any event, clear that Jazīrī and his contemporaries took a dim view of such behavior.

Entertainers and Performers

As coffeehouses proliferated and proprietors vied with one another to draw in customers, many sought to gain a competitive advantage by bringing in live entertainment. Quite often this meant a story-teller, who merely recited or provided himself with modest musical accompaniment on a stringed instrument. Such performers had certain advantages over the other sorts of entertainers whom we shall presently discuss. First, they came cheap. The coffeehouse proprietor had to spend very little out of his own purse to provide such entertainment: in return for his performances, the management sometimes gave the entertainer a meager remuneration. In other circumstances, the coffeehouse owner did not have to pay for such services at all; he merely provided a forum for the performer's eloquence, which was rewarded by voluntary contributions of a few coins apiece from the customers. Even this, though customary, was in no way obligatory. Second, these performances were in scale more practical and better suited to the physical size of the coffeehouse than those of jugglers, groups of musicians, or dancers. Even the meanest coffee shop could, during Ramaḍān especially, have such a story-teller to attract patrons. In such circumstances, he would sit on the front *maṣṭaba* (stoop) and the listeners would arrange themselves on the *maṣṭabas* of the opposite or adjacent shops, or in the narrow confines of the shop itself. The third advantage of such entertainments was that story-tellers were, compared with many other kinds of entertainment, generally considered more wholesome. The works performed were usually old romances, such as stories of 'Antara and the like, or folk tales. Local tastes probably did much to dictate the material: in Persian coffeehouses (later converted almost entirely into teahouses), selections from the *Shāhnāme* were popular. The reciters seem to have been of diverse backgrounds. Some, such as impoverished students or scholars, practiced part-time to supplement their less profitable pursuits. Others were professionals: Evliyā Çelebi speaks of their professional organizations participating in guild processions. At times, it seems, some would give such performances not out of need, but merely to entertain themselves.[41]

Puppet shows of various types also figured among the dramatic entertainments. Russell, who was clearly not very impressed with the coffeehouse nor with its clientele, tells of "an obscene, low kind of puppet-show" that was featured especially during the time of Ramaḍān.[42] The shows were apparently quite popular, but not particularly pleasing to European tastes, as shown in Niebuhr's description of such a performance in Cairo:

> The exhibition is represented upon a very narrow stage, a sort of box which a single person can easily carry about, and into which the performer goes. He sends forward his figures through holes in the coffer, and makes them perform the necessary movements by means of wires passing through the grooves in the lid of the box. With an instrument in his mouth, he gives his voice a shrillness answerable to the size of the figures. The whole together might merit attention, were not the pieces, which the taste of the spectators in Cairo requires to be performed, absolutely execrable. The puppets begin by paying compliments, quarrel by degrees, and end with beating one another.[43]

Undoubtedly the Karagöz type of shadow-play was also popular in the coffeehouses. Niebuhr tells of "magic lanthorn" performances in Cairo. These he found offensive because "their scope was always to turn the dress and manners of the Europeans into ridicule."[44] Performances of a more energetic kind were given by tumblers and jugglers.[45] These, obviously, were probably restricted to the larger, more elaborate sort of establishment.

The entertainments thus far mentioned can be said to have fallen, except in the eyes of the most acutely critical, into the category of harmless, wholesome fun. There was little in the performances of the story-teller or puppeteer—unless Russell is taken to imply lewdness when he called puppet shows "obscene"—to which even the most pious could object. The same cannot be said for some of the other diversions offered in the coffeehouse. Music would have to come, at least in terms of popularity, at the top of the list of less reputable entertainments. From the first, musicians were prominent among the entertainers at the coffeehouse: in Mecca we hear of "drummers and fiddlers" whose presence offended Khā'ir Beg.[46] Though they were considered objectionable by some, the coffeehouse proprietor knew what his public wanted, and gave it to them:

> Generally in the coffeehouses there are many violins, flute players, and musicians, who are hired by the proprietor of the coffeehouse to play and sing much of the day, with the end of drawing in customers.[47]

The coffeehouse with musical entertainment was practically ubiquitous. Aside from Istanbul and the Ḥijāz, coffeehouse musicians are also reported in Egypt, Syria, and Iraq.[48]

This ubiquitousness of music in coffeehouses does not, however, signal universal approval. On the contrary, it is clear from the texts of some of the moral treatises written against the coffeehouse that the presence of music contributed much to the odor of debauchery that made the places so repugnant to the pietistic. Music of a certain type was fine in its place, accompanying civic processions and the like,[49] and military music, as played by the *mehter* bands, was an institution in itself. But music for its own sake, much less as an entertainment for those engaged in other questionable activities, was another matter altogether. It was one of the distinguishing features of many taverns. Even in pre-Islamic times, the wine-house of the Ḥijāz was the scene of musical entertainments and singers were almost always present at wine-bibbing parties. *Ḥadīth* literature records that the Prophet had much to say about music, very little of it favorable. Music taken not only in itself, but in the general atmosphere of revelry to which it did much to contribute, would be doubly damnable.

Who was performing as well as what was being performed no doubt exacerbated the disapproval in many cases. In the early sixteenth century, at least in the Ḥijāz, vocal music was supplied by female as well as male singers. This, of course, was quite in accordance with old revered custom, inasmuch as traditional symposia and meetings of the artistic were held, whether in house or tavern, with the musical accompaniment of songstresses, often demurely screened off from the company, but sometimes mingling more freely with them. Whatever the case may be, many found the custom shocking and repellent. The author of the *Risāla fī aḥkām al-qahwa*, otherwise a supporter of coffee drinking, has nothing but criticism for this sort of activity:

> Perhaps what can be said for prohibiting [coffee] is the evidence that it is drunk in taverns (*ḥānāt*), which embrace all sorts of reprehensible things: singing girls (*qaynāt*), [various types of] fiddles ... the playing of instruments of wanton diversion, dancing, and the clapping of hands.[50]

In Mecca, Khā'ir Beg seemed properly scandalized not only by the presence of musicians but by the fact that these musicians included women as well as men, which doubtless he found indicative of lax morals. From later accounts, it is difficult to tell just how long such songstresses continued to entertain in coffeehouses, nor is it clear that such was ever the case outside the Ḥijāz. It is unlikely that such a holdover from tavern life would have long been tolerated, and one must assume that the more pious would suspect, perhaps with some justification, that vocal performances were not the only services supplied the patrons by such songstresses.[51] Even if this was not the case, the presence of women in the coffeehouse, at least in the capacity of entertainers, was probably an insufferable affront to the social norms of the day. Such behavior might go on in a tavern, whose customers had already abandoned any pretense of respectability, but would be intolerable in a place that had acquired such a large and diverse clientele. In any event, most later accounts make no mention of singing girls. The coffee shop was a world strictly of men.

The lack of female performers could not, of course, eliminate the possibility of the coffeehouse seeming, and in fact being, a place where one's baser desires and proclivities might be indulged. Some coffeehouses indeed appear to have accommodated a variety of sexual tastes. In Baghdad in the early seventeenth century, customers were served coffee from the hands of "pretty boys, richly dressed." George Sandys, writing of Istanbul of roughly the same era, implies a bit more about the rôle of these youths: "Many of the Coffamen [keep] beautifull boyes, who serve as stales to procure them customers."[52] This very quotation is used by the *Oxford English Dictionary* as an example of an archaic use of the word "stale" with the meaning "a deceptive means of allurement; a person or thing held out as a lure or bait to entrap a person." Another obsolete meaning of the word, mentioned in the same entry, is "more fully *common stale*: a prostitute of the lowest class, employed as a decoy by thieves. Often ... used *gen.* as a term of contempt for an unchaste woman." The ambiguity perhaps reflects no desire, conscious or unconscious, on his part to suggest that coffeehouses served as dens for pederastic procurement. Nonetheless Sandys, who was a poet by profession and as such one who could be expected to choose his words carefully, does seem to be trying to imply some sort of unsavory practice, to suggest that the rôle of such boys went beyond that of waiter and busboy. A perhaps clearer statement is that of the author of the *Risāla fī aḥkām al-qahwa*, where he mentions "youths earmarked for the gratification of one's lusts."[53] The other sources, including the Arabic, are silent on this, although it is not impossible that it might be included among the "abominable practices" that often go un-itemized. It should also be noted that there was a certain vague connection between other low-life activities—some of which, such as gambling, are known to have been practiced in coffeehouses—and homosexual tendencies.[54]

Drug Use

Among the factors that dealt a serious blow to the reputation of the coffeehouse was a connection with drug use. It appears that for some reason—chemical or cultural—coffee became a very popular drink among users of certain hard drugs, particularly opium. John Covel, an English clergyman traveling near Izmir in 1670, remarked about "an old *Coffe* man there, who was an *Afionjè* or Ophionjè [Turkish: *afyoncu*], *a great eater of Opium.*"[55] What Covel saw was by no means an isolated coincidence. Kâtib Çelebi tells us, "Drug addicts in particular, finding [coffee] a life-giving thing, which increases their pleasure, were willing to die for a cup."[56]

Drug consumption became one of the activities practiced in the coffeehouse. "The ḳahwagee," Lane tells us, "also keeps two or three narghiles [water pipes] or sheeshehs, and gozes, which latter are used for smoking tumbak [pressed tobacco] ... and ḥasheesh." Russell describes the use of "*sheera*" or "*bing*," which is apparently the leaves of hemp processed into the shape of small lozenges, mixed with tobacco, and used in the narghīla.[57] Actually, it is not at all clear that smoking was the only means by which these drugs were consumed in the coffeehouse. Rosenthal asserts that, any evidence to the contrary for the moment lacking, hashish was eaten rather than smoked before the coming of tobacco to the Middle East in the early seventeenth century.[58] Raymond has also found evidence of the sale of such drugs for consumption in the café, mentioning as well a guild of "sellers of balls of honey mixed with hashish who are at Cairo or Būlāq." Biddulph, in addition, tells of opium being "drunk."[59] While it is possible that he is translating the verb *sh-r-b* literally, this I find unlikely.

Another possible way of interpreting Biddulph's phrase, perhaps the best way, is to assume that he saw opium being drunk with or in coffee. This is not as unlikely as it first sounds, since much evidence exists to suggest such a practice. Rosenthal, discussing the work *Qam' al-wāshīn* (composed no later than A.D. 1583 [A.H. 991]) mentions the passage where the author finds coffee a permissible beverage, unless there are things added to it.[60] What Rosenthal finds cryptic in this allusion is perhaps cleared up by Jazīrī. Among other practices he condemns as polluting and making illegal the use of the otherwise pure drink is "the addition of things to it ... [including] *fāz 'Abbās*."[61] In another place, he sums up his disgust with the situation:

> Aside from hashish, [there are] other [narcotic] pastes that are mixed in [with coffee]. Or one might mix in opium like the paste called *barsh* [another drug preparation] ... , which has become widespread since the [1530s]. Many have been led to ruin by this temptation. They can be reckoned as beasts whom the demons have so tempted.[62]

Jazīrī associates this obvious abomination with the appropriation of the habit by those whose other excesses included many of the activities of the coffeehouse mentioned in the previous pages. Only so many associations can be heaped onto the object of such a dispute before even its strongest advocates find themselves taking a second look at the drink itself and those habits connected with its use that have become current practice.

CHAPTER 8

The Coffeehouse: Social Norms, Social Symbols

Frequently a segment of society will find something objectionable that cannot be attacked by the letter of that society's constitution, be it the revealed word of God, codified habitual practice, or a carefully reasoned system. When asked to produce the legal evidence to support their arguments, these social critics cannot meet the challenge, but this does nothing to diminish their perception that what is going on is, in some way or another, harmful or improper. This attitude does not necessarily make them hypocrites or fanatics, but merely people who perceive a danger to society, even if society does not have the legal armor to defend itself against the peril.

We should not wonder, therefore, if much of what is said attacking coffee or the coffeehouse cannot be backed by citations from the *sharī'a* or even *qānūn* (civil, administrative codes supplementing holy law). By this time it should be clear that the objections are not all directed against the same improprieties, nor are the improprieties all of the same type or level of legal offensiveness. Indeed, at least three distinct categories of objection can be discerned. First there were objections raised against those activities that were conclusively prohibited by the *sharī'a*, activities that were clearly indefensible. These were practices, common to many coffeehouses, that baldly flouted the precepts of the faith, or were at least seen as reprehensible. These we have already seen much in evidence: gambling, drug use, whoring, sodomy, and even musical entertainments must all be considered as running directly contrary to holy law. On the second level, we have those acts that, while in no way contrary to the *sharīʿa*, are thought dangerous for one reason or another. Only in limited circumstances, for instance, could a government demonstrate that the free exchange of ideas in a coffeehouse led to sedition. Nonetheless, plotting in the coffeehouse, or even suspicion of such activity, would obviously be viewed with grave concern by the authorities, and would most likely result in a crackdown of some sort.

As we take up the third category of objection, we pass into a far more murky zone, that of objections on which no real legal action can be taken. What we find here are cases in which there is the intimation of a vague feeling of social uneasiness, a sense that the coffeehouse has somehow affected, for the worse, the behavior of the individual and the community. At times the feelings about the coffeehouse were not unmixed, but on the whole they reflect a sense of social malaise. A late sixteenth-century Turkish traveler in Ottoman Cairo wrote:

> Also [remarkable] is the multitude of coffee-houses in the city of Cairo, the concentration of coffee-houses at every step, and of perfect places where people can assemble. Early rising worshipers and pious men get up and go [there], drink a cup of coffee adding life to their life. They feel, in a way, that its slight exhilaration strengthens them for their religious observance and worship. From that point of view their coffee-houses are commended and praised. But if one considers the ignorant people that assemble in them it is questionable whether they deserve praise. . . .
>
> To make it short, the coffee-houses of Egypt are filled mostly with dissolute persons and opium-eaters. Many of them are occupied

by veteran soldiers, aged officers (*chaushān* and *müteferriqas*). When they arrive in the morning rags and rush mats are spread out, and they stay until evening. Some [of the frequenters of coffeehouses] are drug-users of the slave class; [here follows a section making fun of the Kipchak dialect of these people]. They are a bunch of parasites, *chaushes* and *müteferriqas* by name [only], whose work consists of presiding over the coffee-house, of drinking coffee on credit, talking of frugality, when the matter comes up, and, having told certain matters with all sorts of distortions, of dozing off as soon as the effects of their "grass" subside. In other words, their talk is mostly lies. . . . But no true word ever comes over their lips.[1]

There indeed is stern disapproval here, but few of the practices he names (save the drug use) are actually prosecutable.

What we have in place of holy law as a source for the objections are vague but powerful cultural predilections. Such objections are by far the least tangible, but are at the same time the most interesting, since they can tell us much about the expectations of society, and how perhaps the ultimate success of the institution was the cause, or perhaps only the symptom, of subtle shifts in the framework of that society.

COFFEE AND UNSEEMLY BEHAVIOR

It would be best to begin back with the properties of coffee itself. As has been said, objections to coffee on the basis of its being intoxicating cannot be, and indeed were not, supported by the *sharī'a*, while medical opinion on coffee was so mixed that it could not serve as a reliable basis for prohibition. A curious objection raised by the mid-sixteenth-century Şeyhülislâm Abū al-Su'ūd Efendi (1490–1574 [A.H. 896–982]), that coffee was prohibited because the beans are roasted to the point of carbonization, need not be taken too seriously, since other jurists of his time were almost unanimous in their rejection of his argument.[2]

The absence of intoxicating or noxious properties does not, however, exhaust the objections that could be raised to coffee as a substance.

Setting aside the possibility of illicit material being added to the brew of water and coffee, we know that it still does have physical effects on the drinker, dubbed *marqaḥa* by the earliest devotees of the drink. It makes the heart beat faster, and contributes to a feeling, however temporary, of renewed vigor or even euphoria. In large amounts, it can contribute to insomnia and nervousness. It was this feeling of vigor that was the reputed goal of the Sufis who originally used coffee, and it was also what made it popular among others who had to fight off fatigue. The effects of caffeine were doubtless considered to have contributed as well to the proverbially loquacious behavior of the coffeehouse patron, and on this very point coffee seems to run into trouble.

The potential of coffee for impious as well as devout purposes may not seem quite so clear to us in a society where mild sedatives, such as alcohol, are considered the drugs of choice for those participating in bohemian revels. Such a stimulant as coffee is the drink for those times when we must keep alert and with our wits about us, the serious times of work, study, operating machinery, and the like. We would no more consider a cup of coffee a token of vice than we would a glass of milk. Quite the contrary—it is a sign of virtue, a weapon in the arsenal against that lethargy which undermines the work ethic. Islamic society, of course, has no lack of work ethic, if it comes to that: study, pursuing one's craft, and devotional exercise are all considered laudable and very much encouraged. But in addition, there is a sense of proper deportment, far more circumscribed than that of even the most phlegmatic of Western societies, that is linked to an idea of sobriety which excludes not only narcoticized or stupefied behavior, but hyperactive, frenetic activity, loquaciousness and foolish banter as well. The Prophet is reported to have spoken well of taciturnity and moderation in what speech one does use.[3] Such conceptions became part of the accepted standards of behavior. For instance, a tenth-century writer on elegant manners has the following to say on the subject:

> You should know that part of the manner of the man of breeding, of people possessed of learning and intelligence who are characterized by manly virtue and elegance, is paucity of unnecessary speech, a sense of being above pranks and jesting, abandoning the vulgar behavior of silly jokes, and that boisterousness [characterized by] merry wit and buffoonery, for an excess of such clowning debases a man, lowers his social standing, deprives him of his virtue, and corrupts his nobility.[4]

Nor were such values restricted to the classical past. The chronicler Ibn Ṣaṣrā (wrote 1399) thought it vital enough to digress and devote a short section in his work on fourteenth-century Damascus to the practical and moral importance of taciturnity.[5] In a society where such guidelines are based merely on respect for communal tradition and a sense of how things are done, the person who seriously offends the standards of conduct of the circles in which he travels might find himself viewed as something of an outcast. Where a certain type of behavior is not only considered bad form but also the subject of brisk attacks in the guise of tradition of the Prophet, and where the action is a violation of an all-encompassing code of manly virtue, something that induces such behavior must inevitably be looked on with considerable distaste.

We of course must assume that men went to the coffeehouse to enjoy themselves, but, in the minds of many, the line between enjoying oneself and unseemly behavior was very fine indeed. One of the causes of Jazīrī's consternation with contemporary trends in coffee use was that assemblies where it was drunk had become forums for jesting and amusement. To one of Jazīrī's mind, in a curious parallel with opinion on wine mentioned above, *niya* (intention) was apparently everything. If the goal in seeking stimulation from coffee was laudable, such as study, or, even more so, *dhikr*, then the drink as a means to such an end was unobjectionable. If the desired goal, or even the result, was mere diversion, its use was obviously culpable.[6]

THE IMPORTANCE OF GESTURE: PASSING AROUND THE CUP

Apart from what might be considered that unseemly behavior in the coffeehouse possibly attributed to caffeine, other aspects present themselves in those criticisms of the coffeehouse that were not based on demonstrably illicit activity. It is in this area that we begin to see fully the importance of gesture, of opposition arising against coffee because of certain activities connected with it which aroused indistinct feelings of impropriety, either by traceable connection to some illicit act or owing to something that merely struck the wrong chord in the minds of the arbiters of morals of the age.

A good example of such an objection can be found in the controversy over "passing around the cup" (*idārat al-ka's*) when drinking coffee. This habit, not much in vogue in the coffeehouse in later times, apparently was quite common in the early sixteenth century. It is mentioned in many places by Jazīrī, and according to Kâtib Çelebi was practiced in the coffeehouses of Istanbul as well: "the fact that it is drunk in gatherings, passed hand to hand," he says, "is suggestive of loose-living."[7] Such circulation of a common cup is the subject of almost unanimous disapproval, both by Jazīrī and by his even more critical contemporaries. The description of clandestine activities of those early drinkers in Mecca includes mention of them passing around the cup and taking turns from it (wa-ma'ahum ka's yudīrūnahu wa-yatadāwalūnahu baynahum).[8] Criticism of such action figures prominently in the decision against the drink expressed in the text of the legal question sent to Cairo. Even those otherwise favorably disposed to coffee betray disapproval of the habit of passing the cup. The author of the *Risāla fī aḥkām al-qahwa* condemns the practice of "passing [coffee] around like an intoxicant."[9] Ibn 'Abd al-Ghaffār, in questioning the plausibility of the story of the drinkers at the Sacred Mosque in Mecca, notes how odd it was that men should go to all the trouble of preparing for and performing a celebration of the *mawlid* of the Prophet, and then:

> After, or even during [the celebration of the *mawlid*], the person in charge of the gathering has brought for them a drink, which they pass around among themselves in the manner of an intoxicant, the act of passing around the wine [cup], resembling [the activities of] the licentious.[10]

So strong was this association that one scholar, who caused himself a tremendous amount of trouble at the assembly of ulema at Mecca in 1511, and who was even mentioned as an object of possible chastisement in the letter to Cairo, came to all this grief by merely suggesting that passing around the cup was not in itself reprehensible, since the Prophet himself had done so. His shocked colleagues dismissed this argument, since the passing of coffee resembled the way wine was passed around, and in no way was similar to the purported activities of the Prophet. Of the major writers on coffee, only the author of the *Iṣṭifā' al-ṣafwa* does not find passing the cup essentially reprehensible: if one is not trying to resemble a wine drinker, it is acceptable, even laudable, but if one is, then it is not proper.[11]

The evil associations with the simple act of passing around a cup can be traced back several centuries. In the time of the Prophet there seems to have been little prejudice against the act. There are indeed *ḥadīths* in which the Prophet passes a cup, the theme of these all being generally that the Prophet is given something to drink, and after drinking passes the cup to the right, even though on his left is a person of some eminence (usually Abū Bakr) and on his right is a youth or a Bedouin. This is all to demonstrate that the person on the right always has precedence in such activities.[12] By the ninth century, however, there was already a serious taint on the passing of cups:

> Al-Quṭay'ī said: "'Abd Allāh ibn Dā'ūd said to me: 'There is no harm if a man drinks [*nabīdh*] to wash down his food, just as one would drink water [for that purpose].' And he said: 'It is reprehensible to pass around the cup. . . .' And he said: 'The testimony of the man who passes the cup is not admissible.'"[13]

It is not clear how such an attitude arose, although from the context of the objections to passing the coffee cup it would seem that the act was commonly associated with wine drinking in groups.[14] If so, it is equally unclear whether it was the mere act of circulating the cup among the drinkers, or more specific similarities in the way the cup was passed, how the revelers acted toward one another and the like that is referred to when it is said that people drank coffee in the manner of drinking wine. The importance of one's manner of drinking, even if only symbolic, is clear from the following *fatwā*:

> [Al-Ramlī] was asked about a gathering where they drank something permitted, and passed it around among them as one would pass around wine. If they did not intend to liken themselves to wine drinkers, is that activity forbidden or not? He answered that their drinking it in the described manner was not forbidden, but rather that it was forbidden if they intended emulation of wine drinkers.[15]

It is neither the substance that they drank nor any punishable offense that led to complaints over this aspect of coffee drinking. It is merely that this act, and probably others even less discernible and hence uncatalogued, lent a general air of debauchery to the proceedings. Such activity would not really be in the province of the *qāḍī* to control (although a zealous *muḥtasib* might feel compelled to take action); it was the atmosphere, the vague feeling of a debauched frolic, that such subtle gestures called to mind that was behind much of the opposition to the coffeehouse.

LEISURE, SLOTH, AND LITERATURE

Another image commonly associated with the coffeehouse is that of leisure. Whether the activity there was of a dissolute and debauched nature or not, one thing is clear: our sources do not consider it productive. From the tone of what Muṣṭafā ʻAlī said about Cairene coffeehouses, the idleness of the habitué was in no way laudable. As coffeehouses proliferated, Kâtib Çelebi tells us, "working for one's living fell into disfavour."[16] The picture often given is that of the appearance of a class of regular clientele, without any visible means of support, who haunt the cafés, smoking, sipping coffee, conversing, and otherwise diverting themselves. One traveler in the end of the sixteenth century tells of a class of men "passing the day banqueting and carousing, drinking a certaine liquor which they do call *Coffe*."[17] Gianfrancesco Morosini, in the same era, emphasizes the atmosphere of indolence, telling of them passing their time "in grandissimo ozio."[18] To these "young idlers," as D'Ohsson calls them, lounging around the coffeehouse seems to have become a profession rather than a pastime. Even if they are engaged in nothing as harmful and disreputable as gambling and drug use, such conduct can be deplorable in the eyes of society as a whole. The passage from the eleventh-century writers Miskawayh and al-Tawḥīdī that Rosenthal quotes in reference to gaming can well be applied to the activities of the coffeehouse as a whole:

> "Doing nothing (*'uṭlah*) is bad, and reason shuns it. Therefore, people who have free time (*al-furrāgh*) occupy themselves with playing chess and *nard*, notwithstanding the stupidity of those games and useless waste of one's life and time that goes with them. Voluntarily sitting around unoccupied and motionless is detested by all people." [Rosenthal adds:] However, the philosopher no doubt was of the opinion that, even if no practical work is waiting to be done, time can always be employed usefully with thinking.[19]

Sitting around in the coffeehouse would not, it is clear, be by such standards an acceptable way to pass one's time.

Even the literary activity that is said in some sources to have pervaded many of these places would probably not be sufficient to salvage their reputations. For one thing, the reading of newly composed verses might, like the performances of musicians, call to mind the wine-bibbing party. Literary activity in such a setting at the court may have added much to the cultural heritage, while harming nobody, but while the elite at court could be wary of their own souls, the democratization of such goings-on, their rapid spread among a vast segment of the community, might be seen as a breakdown of social morality on a grand scale.

To make matters worse, such literary activity was, from all descriptions, profane. One gets the feeling that there was the sense in some quarters that the worldly activity of the coffeehouse had come in part to replace scholarly study and contemplation in the mosque. Whereas formerly men might have spent their time studying or conversing on subjects of significance to their souls in the mosque, now they went to the coffeehouse, a place where little in the way of pious activity went on. Perhaps indicative of the presence of such feelings is the list given by D'Ohsson of those who first and most vigorously opposed coffee drinking: while some of the most loyal patrons of the coffeehouse were teachers, judges, and other men of law—that is men of considerable learning in the religious sphere—its opponents he portrays as "shaykhs, imams, and muezzins," those who might be labeled, at least in part, as mosque functionaries. This distinction was to become even more clear: when Abū al-Su'ūd Efendi issued his famous proclamation against coffee, his contemporaries and colleagues raced almost to a man to deny the validity of his arguments. But minor religious functionaries, men whose chief business was the spiritual activities of the general public at the mosque rather than exposition on detailed questions of law, seem to have perceived the coffeehouse as cutting into their territory. One indication the coffeehouse might have been stealing some of the customers of the mosque was the very popularity of the places during Ramaḍān. Men seem to have in part chosen to spend their after-dark hours at the coffee shop instead of at the mosque.

THE COFFEEHOUSE AND COGNATE INSTITUTIONS

This leads us to the question of what, if anything, the coffeehouse replaced in the social lives of the community. Did it merely take over some of the functions of a pre-existing institution, or did it represent something entirely new, either as the answer to a growing demand in a community undergoing some sort of social change, or something that instigated change itself?

On the tavern much has already been said. In many ways the coffeehouse bears the greatest resemblance to it, particularly as regards the concomitant activities. Coffee's critics, with the object of establishing a damning relationship between the places, were among the first to point out the similarities. There was, however, that one fundamental difference: taverns sold wine, and hence were by essence disreputable, while coffeehouses sold coffee, a drink that was not demonstrably illegal. The same distinction must be drawn between the coffeehouse and gambling dens and other spots of night life, whose mass appeal could never, for the same reason as given for taverns, fully develop.

There was another institution, particularly popular in the Turkish part of the empire, whose legal and social status was somewhat ambiguous. This was the *bozahane*. That they were of very questionable reputation is demonstrated by Evliyā Efendi's description of a survey and imperial review of all major guilds ordered by Murat IV in 1638 (A.H. 1048):

> He gave the command that the guild Buza-makers should pass last of all, and no inn-keepers be found in the Imperial camp. [Murat said:] "They shall assist the Buza-makers ... in the procession; they shall not be allowed to play like the other guilds their eightfold music, but pass only with cymbals and drums; it shall be known on this occasion how many Buza- and wine-houses there are, and how many inn-keepers."[20]

This was bad company indeed to be thrown in with. *Boza* is a drink actually closer to a solid than a liquid, resembling nothing more than cool, slightly fermented farina, with a sort of fizzy tingle imparted by the carbon dioxide produced during fermentation. The presence of this carbon dioxide, as well as the tell-tale yeasty-sour smell and taste of the stuff, leaves little doubt that it contains some, though probably very little, alcohol. This in itself would not be sufficient to declare it forbidden, since it is made from grain and not grapes. *Boza*, or *Vefa bozası* (so named after a district in Istanbul famous for its *bozahanes*) is still sold today, strangely enough in sweet shops and ice cream parlors. In any event, the *bozahane* seems to have come off little better than the tavern in the social scale.

Another institution, which in some ways resembled the coffeehouse, was the public bath. It has been mentioned earlier that it may have provided women with much the same opportunity for socializing as the coffeehouse did for men. Actually, to men of the leisured classes as well the bath could be a place where one went and spent a considerable amount of time in social contact with a variety of people. Even some of the illicit activities of the coffeehouse, such as the use of hashish, went on in the bath as well.[21] With time coffee itself came to be offered as refreshment for bathers.[22] But in essence the two institutions were vastly different. For one thing, the bath could not offer the range and variety of diversions that the coffeehouse could. There is no mention of live entertainments at the baths, nor of gambling. Secondly, the coffeehouse appears to have become, as the elaborate bath could not (except for the very wealthy) a part of one's everyday routine.

Finally, as a locus for conversations and restful contemplation, the coffeehouse in some ways paralleled the functions of the mosque. But again, it was a place where one could indulge in a level of conviviality and diversion which would have been unseemly, if not sacreligious, in the latter. Though both served as forums for study or literary pursuits, the coffeehouse could act as host and stage to a far more profane and worldly artist. Nor did the mosque cater to one's tastes for music and other more impious entertainments.

If the coffeehouse shared many characteristics with these pre-existing institutions, then, it was still no mere amalgam or hybrid, but rather something radically different from what had gone before. In its introduction and success we can discern elements of change in social interaction and social symbolism. These last may account for the early and persistent opposition to it.

Up until the appearance of the coffeehouse, night life in the city was limited either to the tavern or gambling den, where one went at the peril of one's soul, reputation or perhaps life, and various loci of religious activity, either the Sufi meeting, if one belonged, or, on special occasions, the mosque. One did not risk eternal torment through frequenting these latter places, but one found very little in the way of worldly pleasure, either. The coming of the coffeehouse signaled the beginning of an entirely new phenomenon. Perfectly respectable people went out at night for purposes other than piety. Men were now offered the option of going to a semirespectable establishment and amusing themselves with conversation and diversions of various degrees of innocence.

In still another sense the coffeehouse was an innovation that might have rubbed against the grain of accepted practice. Restaurants where one sat and ate were almost totally lacking up to this point. S. D. Goitein mentions the existence of a variety of take-out establishments in medieval Cairo, but, as he points out, no respectable person would ever sit and consume the meal there, but rather would take it home.[23] Now it became acceptable practice to go and sit and comsume coffee, all day long and well into the night if one so wished. It is no wonder that such an innovation, combined with what has already been alluded to concerning the occasional transferral of the act of hospitality from the home to the coffeehouse, caused in some an uncertain, nagging feeling of social malaise.

EATING, DRINKING, AND SOCIAL CHANGE

What in retrospect appears as a relatively minor change in the patterns of everyday life must, at the time they originally appeared, have seemed to some a disruption of the natural order of things. To a greater or lesser extent we all have, through the process of acculturation that begins almost at birth, a sense of the proper way things are to be done: how one behaves; what activities are acceptable; what the proper relationship with one's family, friends, acquaintances, and strangers is; how we associate with the rest of society. A change, no matter how subtle, in this network of social relationships and habits is perceptible, although the way different people react to this perception varies greatly. Some accept it, some revel in it, while others, either because of the depth of their reverence for tradition or because they have received their set of social norms linked to a greater system of ethics or religious belief, view such a disruptive shift as a threat (of greater or lesser danger) to the order of things as they should be. Egregious or alarming behavior is instantly recognized and reacted to, but even subtle shifts, in no way demonstrably harmful, in the patterns or social life touch nerves and elicit responses from the acutely traditional, although they might not even be aware of the source of their anxiety, but tend to attribute it to the most easily identifiable symbol or cause of the change.

When coffee and the coffeehouse were introduced, the changes that they triggered or symptomized provoked a variety of reactions. Those most deeply troubled had little difficulty finding some aspect of the situation to which they could attribute their alarm—surely there were enough objectively dangerous practices associated with the café—but these were accidental attributes of the place. In essence, the coffeehouse was a new locus of social intercourse, in which new patterns of social behavior were manifested.

Few human activities are more basic than eating. The person deprived of human companionship, sexual relations, creative outlets, or one of a variety of other activities considered essential to the human condition may wither, but deprived of food, he dies. Eating is a practice around which we have built ring after ring of cultural associations, so that what we eat, how we eat, with whom we eat, and where we eat are all very much determined by, and in some way determine, who we are. In our practice of this most vital function we reflect millennia of cultural influences, and a shift in these habits is indicative of a change in cultural orientation, or at least in mental outlook.

Eating is also a particularly social activity, perhaps going back to the days when food moved and fought back, so that we needed the aid of our fellows to subdue and prepare it. It is hard to say whether it is a universal phenomenon, but at very least it is one that the West shares with the Islamic Near East, that there seems something a trifle unnatural about habitually taking our meals alone. Usually in our lives this originates with us eating at home with our families, first as dependents, later as providers, and perhaps still later as dependents again. It is probably no accident that the hearth is a symbol of home and family in a great variety of cultures.

As we have seen, there was little in the way of restaurant patronage in the Near East in the sixteenth century (in many places today there is still none): meals were taken at home, and whatever entertaining one did was also at home. The relationship of host and guest established a very intimate, almost a sacred bond. It is impossible to assume that such relationships could undergo a shift, no matter how slight, without it reflecting a change in the way people socialized on a very basic level. And yet this is exactly what happened with the introduction of coffee.

On a variety of levels, the introduction of coffee and the coffeehouse signaled a change in the life in the cities of the Islamic eastern Mediterranean in the sixteenth century. On the most basic level, the change is obvious, in that a new foodstuff, hitherto unknown, had come into great favor with persons of all stations. It provided new professions, new sources of income, renewed revenues from trade.

The commodity was also responsible for a change in the face of the city, for it gave birth to a new institution, in many ways unlike anything that had ever been seen before. New smells, those of roasting and brewing coffee, pervaded the streets and marketplaces. And where formerly the lights at night burned mostly from the mosque, and there usually only at times of festival, the lights burned far into the night in the coffeehouses.

More importantly, those lights burned because the coffeehouses were packed with people. In earlier times, there were few and particular reasons for a person to be out at night. The mosque drew occasional crowds after dark at certain times of the year, and to some extent the Sufi orders were nightly meeting places for the followers of their discipline. Other than that, only the taverns, gambling houses, and other dens of spiritual perdition drew their patrons. If one mixed and mingled with one's friends, one did so by being host or guest at a private residence.

The coffeehouse did much to change this. Men went out at night to drink, meet with others, exchange information, ideas, or pleasantries, and otherwise amuse themselves. Hospitality was no longer synonymous with the home, nor was one's list of leisure-time companions coterminous with one's familiars from other contexts. To some extent the divisions of quarters in large cities may have been undermined physically, socially, and perhaps psychologically by the centrally located coffeehouses in which persons from many areas congregated. Even activities that had been looked on with some disapproval became with time and familiarity in the coffeehouse somewhat less sinister: the backgammon board is hardly looked on as a tool of Satan anymore. In essence, new dimensions had been added to the social life of the city.

An examination of the reaction to the appearance of the coffeehouse is useful not only because of what insights it might provide concerning changes in society at that time, but also because it provides a good case study of the mechanisms and dynamics involved in that society reacting to, dealing with, and eventually accommodating change. Most interesting is the apparent adaptability and flexibility of the ultimate "constitution" of the society, the *sharīʿa*, in the face of a new question. In spite of what is considered the stagnation of that system of laws after the so-called "closing of the gates of *ijtihād* [independent juridical interpretation]" in the tenth century, the framework of the *sharīʿa* did not give shelter to the culturally conservative. Quite the contrary: while many of the foremost opponents of coffee or the coffeehouse came from the ranks of the religious elite, many other guardians of the law, the party which in the end prevailed, affirmed the principle that the burden of proof lay with those who wished to take action to stop the spread of the habit. That is to say, they affirmed that the new objects of discussion could not be prohibited unless the opponents could prove that in some positive way such practices were directly contrary to the *sharīʿa*. If the case at hand is in any way indicative, the existence of any damaging principle of *bidʿa*, of the idea that because something is an innovation it is by necessity suspicious and blameworthy, is a myth. At the very least, the principle of *bidʿa* is subordinate to that of *al-ibāḥa al-aṣlīya*. One must prove an innovation is illegal, otherwise it is legal.

And in fact, what was originally innovation has become, in the past four centuries, an integral part of social life. The view of the society as stagnant, immutable over the millennia, is a gross distortion. The fact is that where there had been no coffeehouses, they appeared and flourished, and the changes that they brought with them remained as well. The pattern of social life as it existed in the fourteenth century was no longer the pattern by the seventeenth, a change both wrought and symptomized by the success and longevity of the institution of the coffeehouse.

APPENDIX

Note on Sources

The greater part of the works cited in this book have been published, and will be familiar to many. A few, however—and these include some of the works of greatest importance to the study—exist only in manuscript form, or at best in incomplete editions or translations. Here I should like to make a few comments concerning these unpublished, and hence generally inaccessible, works.

By far the most extensive and ambitious of the extant sixteenth-century treatises on coffee is the work of Zayn al-Dīn 'Abd al-Qādir ibn Muḥammad al-Anṣārī al-Jazīrī al-Ḥanbalī, the *'Umdat al-ṣafwa fī ḥill al-qahwa*. It is not only the most impressive in terms of size (running to some sixty-eight folios in the Paris manuscript), but in scope as well. The work, like those of practically all other sixteenth-century writers on coffee, is essentially polemical: the reader is seldom able to lose sight of the fact that Jazīrī is writing to justify the use of coffee. But he is not merely concerned with the narrow parameters of the legal argument. Much of the first chapter, itself longer than most other treatises on coffee, is concerned with the history of coffee drinking, from its initial introduction in the Yemen to the mid-sixteenth century. This is not, of course, disinterested scholarship, since the end of much of this historical discussion is to point out the folly of the various attempts at prohibition. His own opinions aside, however, Jazīrī's work is the most comprehensive and useful of the sixteenth-century essays on coffee.

Carl Brockelmann in the *Geschichte der arabischen Literatur* (*GAL*), 2:325, lists three existing manuscripts of the *'Umdat al-ṣafwa* in European libraries, at Paris (Bibliothèque nationale no. 4590), Madrid (Escurial no. 1170), and Gotha (cat. Pertsch no. 2106), and one at Alexandria. Of these, I have made use of those from Paris and Madrid. The former is written in clear, if somewhat messy, *naskh*, while the latter is in somewhat neater *naskh*, but has far more copyist's errors and omissions. Two partial translations of this work have been made by European scholars, both working from the Paris manuscript. In the late seventeenth century, Antoine Galland did a partial translation, which served as the core of his work *De l'origine et progrès du café* (Caen, 1699). In the early nineteenth century, Antoine Isaac Silvestre de Sacy edited the first two chapters and part of the seventh and supplied a translation, with an impressive amount of annotation, for his tuitional *Chrestomathie arabe* (2d ed., Paris, 1826). Throughout this work, I have adopted the practice of referring to de Sacy's edition where feasible; for references to sections that he did not edit, or where I believe there to be a mistake in edition, translation, or annotation in de Sacy's work, I also refer to the folios of the manuscripts.

Establishing the date when Jazīrī wrote the *'Umdat al-ṣafwa* is a bit of a problem, based on discrepancies between the Paris and Escurial manuscripts. The Escurial manuscript (folio 11v) gives the date of composition as 966 (A.D. 1558–59), while the Paris manuscript (folio 8v) gives it as 996 (A.D. 1587–88). This may well be due to a copyist's mistake in one of the manuscripts, since in a sloppy original the words *sittīn* (sixty) and *tis'īn* (ninety) might easily be confused. De Sacy, who prepared his edition solely from the Paris manuscript, was aware that the Escurial manuscript was dated 966, and therefore concluded that the Paris manuscript was a later edition revised by the author. This theory he reinforced with the fact that in the Paris manuscript (folio 11v) Jazīrī records the date of A.H. 993 for the death of the scholar Sa'd al-Dīn 'Alī ibn Muḥammad ibn al-'Arrāq. This, I am afraid, only confuses the issue. The Escurial manuscript (folio 15v) gives the date of his death as 963, again bringing up the *sittīn/tis'īn* problem. Fortunately, in this case we have some outside confirmation from Ibn al-'Imād (*Shadharāt al-dhahab*, 8:337) who notes that Sa'd al-Dīn 'Alī, a son of Muḥammad ibn al-'Arrāq, died in A.H. 963. (However, even here there is some confusion since the Paris manuscript has the incomplete word *awlā*, which de Sacy assumes to be *awliyā'* [disciples], but which is clearly *awlād* [sons] in the Escurial manuscript.) This does not completely solve the problem of dating the manuscripts, since it merely demonstrates that the Paris manuscript was not *necessarily* written after A.H. 993, but it does throw some doubt on de Sacy's theory that the Paris manuscript is a revised version. Indeed, except for the usual number of copyist's errors, there are few significant differences between the two manuscripts.

About Jazīrī himself we know precious little. Brockelmann (*GAL*, 2:325; *Supplement*, 2:447) lists two other works by him, one on the pilgrimage and routes to Mecca, and one on the virtues and excellences of the Arabs. From his names, as de Sacy points out, we can learn a bit about him: he was from the Arabian Peninsula, of Medinian origin, and belonged to the Ḥanbalī school of jurisprudence. Although by most indications, including internal evidence in the *'Umdat al-ṣafwa*, he resided in Cairo, it is clear that he made frequent trips to the Ḥijāz. In addition, and of special importance to the question at hand, he was, if not himself an active member of a Sufi order, a man with strong connections to Sufism and acquainted with many of the Sufi luminaries of his day.

Jazīrī's work, important as it may be, is not entirely original. He quotes extensively from other authors, particularly from the man who appears to be the true father of literature on coffee, one Shihāb al-Dīn Aḥmad ibn 'Abd al-Ghaffār. Ibn 'Abd al-Ghaffār's work on coffee is apparently lost, but we do know something about him. Brockelmann, who says he wrote around 1530, mentions two works of his, a commentary on the *Fann al-'arabīya wa-ta'alluqātuhu* by the renowned fifteenth-century scholar Suyūṭī (d. 1505 [A.H. 911]), and his own *Izālat al-ghishā' 'an ḥukm ṭawf al-nisā' ba'd al-'ishā'*. Brockelmann describes the contents of the latter work as being "against the prohibition, that women might no longer leave their houses after sundown, and especially that they are no longer permitted to set foot in the mosques—this [prohibition] being an offensive innovation" (*GAL*, 2:387). Like his work on coffee, it seems to be essentially a polemic, and on a similar theme—prohibitions of things not expressly prohibited are themselves essentially wicked. Large portions of Ibn 'Abd al-Ghaffār's work on coffee appear not only in the *'Umdat al-ṣafwa*, but elsewhere, such as in the *Risāla fī aḥkām al-qahwa*. Another writer whom Jazīrī frequently cites is Fakhr al-Dīn Abū Bakr ibn Abī Yazīd al-Makkī, about whom we know very little. Jazīrī furnishes us with the title of al-Makkī's treatise on coffee, the *Ithārat al-nakhwa bi-ḥill al-qahwa*; but beyond this title, of which Brockelmann makes no mention in the *GAL*, the details of al-Makkī's life and career remain obscure.

The *Risāla fī aḥkām al-qahwa*, in the Staatsbibliothek der Preußischer Kulturbesitz in Berlin (cat. Ahlwardt no.

5476) presents us with a bit of a problem. Although attributed to Suyūṭī, internal evidence points to the contrary. Particularly telling is the fact that the work contains lengthy extracts from the writings of Ibn ʻAbd al-Ghaffār. On the one hand, there are passages that make it clear that Ibn ʻAbd al-Ghaffār was present in Cairo in the beginning of the tenth century A.H., when Suyūṭī was still alive and living in the same city. On the other hand, Brockelmann (*GAL*, 2:387), in reference to a different work, speaks of Ibn ʻAbd al-Ghaffār writing in 1530 (A.H. 937), twenty-five years after Suyūṭī's death. More conclusive, however, is the fact that much of what Ibn ʻAbd al-Ghaffār has to say in his work about coffee indicates that he wrote sometime after the first decade of the tenth century A.H., that is to say, after Suyūṭī's death. How much later is difficult to establish, but it is clear from the *ʻUmdat al-ṣafwa* (ms. Paris, fol. 17v; ms. Escurial, fol. 23r) that it was composed after the Meccan incident of 1511 (A.H. 917), since Ibn ʻAbd al-Ghaffār makes frequent allusion to it. In light of this fact, one cannot help but view the authorship of the *Risāla fī aḥkām al-qahwa* as uncertain. It is again a clearly pro-coffee work, in which the author does, however, carefully disassociate himself from suspicion of approval of the less savory aspects of coffeehouse life.

The manuscript of the sixteenth-century work *Qamʻ al-wāshīn fī dhamm al-barrāshīn* by Nūr al-Dīn Abū al-Ḥasan ʻAlī Ibn al-Jazzār, is found at the Bibliothek der Rijksuniversiteit, Leiden (cat. de Jong and de Goeje no. 1880 [cod. 814[12] Warn.], fols. 273r–84r). This is, in fact, not a work specifically about coffee at all, rather it deals with the harmfulness of the narcotic preparation *barsh*, and has been cited extensively by Franz Rosenthal in his important study on the use of hashish, *The Herb* (Leiden: E. J. Brill, 1971). Ibn al-Jazzār did not, however, confine himself to a discussion of *barsh*, but chose to devote the last few pages of his work to coffee, which he found licit as long as it was not adulterated with illegal substances.

An entirely different approach, one based on and almost exclusively dealing with received medical wisdom on coffee, is that of Muḥammad ibn Maḥmūd ibn Burhān al-Dīn al-Zaynī al-Ḥusaynī, a sixteenth-century physician about whom very little is known. His short treatise on the harmful effects of coffee is contained in a manuscript at Princeton, Yahuda collection, cat. Mach no. 2082.

The *Iṣṭifā' al-ṣafwa li-taṣfiyat al-qahwa* (ms. Leiden, cat. de Jong and de Goeje no. 1872 [cod. 1138 Warn.]) is an odd little treatise. The authorship of the work is uncertain and it is listed in the catalogue as anonymous, although van Arendonk ("Ḳahwa," *Encyclopaedia of Islam*, 2d ed.) does attempt to establish the authorship. In any event, it most definitely dates from the sixteenth century. The manuscript is nineteen folios in length in clear, legible *naskh*. An unabashed defense of the use of coffee, it is in many places written in the first person, with coffee itself as the narrator.

GLOSSARY

al-Ahzar: mosque and important center for study of Islamic theology and law in Cairo, founded by the Fāṭimids in 972 (A.H. 361).

bid'a: an innovation, a novelty; specifically a harmful or religiously suspect innovation; the opposite of *sunna* (q.v.).

bit': mead; an alcoholic beverage, particularly popular in the Yemen, made of fermented honey.

bunn: (1) coffee beans; (2) specifically, the kernel of the coffee bean, as opposed to its husk.

dhikr: lit., remembrance or mention; specifically, remembrance and mention of the name and glory of God; later that set ritual for the praise of God and attainment of nearness to God performed by various Sufi orders.

dhimmīs: more formally *ahl al-dhimma*: those belonging to the "protected peoples"—usually Christians and Jews. In exchange for payment of a head tax (*jizya*) and acceptance of certain social disadvantages by these minorities, Islam guarantees freedom from molestation, enslavement, seizure of property, and the like.

faqīh (pl. *fuqahā'*): one learned in the details of the holy law.

fatwā (pl. *fatāwā*): an opinion on a specific point of law drawn up by a mufti (q.v.), usually at the request of one of the participants in a legal conflict or an individual seeking guidance for proper conduct. Unlike the judgment of a *qāḍī* (q.v.), a *fatwā* carries no legal weight in itself, but is nonetheless taken into consideration when a ruling is given. Naturally, the greater the stature and reputation of the mufti, the greater the weight of his legal opinion.

ḥadīth (pl. *aḥādīth*): a tradition, a precedent; specifically, a report of a deed or statement of the Prophet or one of his immediate companions, taken as a guide to proper behavior, and as a source of holy law, generally second only to a direct Qur'ānic statement.

Ḥanafī: one of the four major schools of *sunnī* jurisprudence, or an adherent of that school. Following the teachings of the eighth-century Iraqi legal scholar Abū Ḥanīfa and his pupil Abū Yūsuf (d. 798 [A.H. 182]), the school allowed the frequent use of individual rationalist interpretation. It was the official legal school of the Ottoman state.

Ḥanbalī: one of the four major schools of *sunnī* jurisprudence, or an adherent thereof. The school is named after the jurist Aḥmad ibn Ḥanbal (780–855 [A.H. 164–241]). It puts particular stress on *ḥadīth* (q.v.) as a source of law, and admits independent reasoning only in extreme cases.

al-ibāḥa al-aṣlīya: legal theory of "original permissibility," that is, if something is not explicitly prohibited by one of the *sharī'a*, it is permitted.

ibrīq: coffee pot, or, more generally, any small vessel for liquid designed for easy pouring—e.g., a pitcher or ewer. The more common term used in Turkey for the familiar tinned brass or copper coffee pot is now *cezve.*

ijmāʿ: consensus; specifically, the consensus of men of legal learning on the Islamic community as a whole or of a particular area. Since it was deemed impossible for the community as a whole to agree on a religious error, *ijmāʿ* was regarded by many schools of jurisprudence as a valid source of law.

ijtihād: the application of individual reason to the basic sources of the *sharīʿa*, using one's own powers of independent thought and analogy (*qiyās*) to derive legal principles not so much from handbooks of practical jurisprudence (*furūʿ*), but directly from Qur'ān and *sunna* (q.v.).

khamr: wine; specifically wine as covered by the legal prohibition, that beverage that is expressly prohibited by the Qur'ān (5:90–91). The exact definition of *khamr*, and of those beverages regarded as *khamr* for the purposes of the law, varies from school to school.

kıraathane: "reading room"; a medium size neighborhood coffee/teahouse, common in Turkey.

madhhab (pl. *madhāhib*): a school of Islamic jurisprudence; especially one of the four mutually tolerant schools of *sunnī* jurisprudence, viz.: the Ḥanafī, Mālikī, Shāfiʿī, and Ḥanbalī.

Mālikī: one of the four major *sunnī* schools of jurisprudence, named after the eighth-century jurist Mālik ibn Anas. It is now the predominant school in North Africa (except Egypt).

manqala: a game, played in coffeehouses from the earliest times, involving the movement and distribution of small counting pieces in twelve (or fourteen) hemispherical hollows on the game board.

marqaḥa: "coffee euphoria"; term in sixteenth-century peninsular Arabic, perhaps of foreign (Ethiopian?) origin, denoting the usual physical and mental effects of coffee.

mawlid: birthday, especially the birthday of the Prophet (more fully *mawlid al-nabī*), a religious festival in which Sufi groups in particular play a large part.

maysir: pre-Islamic Arabian game for stakes, involving the drawing of marked arrows to win shares in a slaughtered camel; later, dicing games in general.

mufti (Arabic *muftī*): jurisconsult; a scholar whose opinion (*fatwā*, q.v.) is sought on a particular point of law. Originally strictly an unofficial position determined solely by one's reputation for learning, under the Ottomans it became an appointed governmental position.

muḥtasib: civic official charged primarily with overseeing the marketplaces, his duties included as well "the encouragement of good and the forbidding of evil," making him something of an arbiter of public morality.

muskir: active participle of the verb *askara* "to make someone drunk." It can be used either as a substantive, "intoxicant," or an adjective, "intoxicating," a distinction of great importance in legal usage—see chapter four.

Mu'tazila: the philosophical-theological movement of the eighth-ninth century A.D., which supported the idea of human free will as opposed to predestination.

nabīdh: wine in its broadest sense; a fermented beverage made from fruits, grains, or other material, such as honey.

qāḍī (pl. *quḍāt*): judge, one who renders an actual official decision on cases involving holy law.

qahwa: coffee; more precisely, the stimulating beverage made from the fruit of the *coffea arabica*.

qahwa bunnīya: the beverage made from the kernels of the fruit (*bunn*) alone, or from the husks and kernels together.

qahwa qishrīya: the beverage made exclusively from the husks (*qishr*, q.v.).

qānūn: civil or administrative codes derived from secular authority. The opposite of the European concept of "canon" law, *qānūn* is comprised of those laws and regulations established by the government that are *not* covered by the *sharī'a* (q.v.).

qāt: kat, the shrub *catha edulis*, whose stimulating leaves are still chewed extensively in the Yemen.

qishr: the husks of the coffee bean, or the beverage prepared exclusively from the husks.

sakrān: drunk; one who meets the legal definition of drunkenness, and is in consequence subject to punishment.

Shāfi'ī: one of the four major *sunnī* schools of jurisprudence, named after the jurist Abū 'Abd Allāh Muḥammad al-Shāfi'ī (767–820 [A.H. 150–204]). It is the predominant legal school of Egypt.

sharī'a: the holy law of Islam, based on Qur'ān, *ḥadīth* (q.v.), consensus of the community (*ijmā'*), and, depending on the school, analogy (*qiyās*).

Sufism: religious movement characterized by an emphasis on the mystical, a personal striving to achieve propinquity and ultimate unity with the Divine.

sukr: intoxication; in legal practice, defined in various ways by the different schools of jurisprudence.

sunna: custom, tradition; standard custom and practice of the community, based primarily on the deeds and sayings of the Prophet and his companions, roughly akin to the Roman concept of *mos maiorum*.

ta'aṣṣub: fanaticism; fierce adherence to a given position (e.g., in an argument).

ulema (Arabic *'ulamā'*; sing. *'ālim*): the knowledgeable; broadly, those men of learning who concern themselves with things religious, particularly the law.

NOTES

CHAPTER TWO

1. Quoted in Ibn al-ʻImād, *Shadharāt al-dhahab fī akhbār man dhahab*, 8 vols. (Cairo, 1350–51/[1931–32]; reprint, Beirut, 1966), 8:40.

2. European writers offer their own version for the use of coffee in antiquity, likening it to the famous "black broth" of the Spartans. Jean de La Roque (*Voyage de l'Arabie Heureuse* [Amsterdam, 1716], p. 265) works to refute another claim, that by Pietro della Valle, that coffee is mentioned by Homer.

3. See ʻAbd al-Qādir ibn Muḥammad al-Anṣārī al-Jazīrī al-Ḥanbalī, *ʻUmdat al-ṣafwa fī ḥill al-qahwa*, ed. Antoine Isaac Silvestre de Sacy, in his *Chrestomathie arabe*, 2d ed., 3 vols. (Paris, 1826), 1:143; ms. Paris (Bibliothèque nationale, arab. no. 4590), fol. 8r; ms. Escurial (cat. Derenbourg no. 1170), fol. 10v.

4. See, among others, Richard Bradley, *A Short Historical Account of Coffee* (London, 1714).

5. "Wa-qulnā lā fī ghayrihi li-anna ẓuhūr al-qahwa fī barr Ibn Saʻd al-Dīn wa-bilād al-Ḥabasha wa-al-Jabart wa-ghayrihā min barr al-ʻAjam fa-lā yuʻlamu matā kāna awwaluhu wa-lā ʻalimnā sababahu." Jazīrī, *ʻUmdat al-ṣafwa*, ed. de Sacy, 1:145. De Sacy, in his notes on this section, explains the derivations of all these names—it is clear enough that we are speaking of Ethiopia. In particular, "ʻAjam" here is used in the general sense of "non-Arab," rather than the more specific and common "Iranian." "Jabart" refers to the Muslim popu-

lation of Ethiopia (see E. Ullendorf, "Djabart," in *The Encyclopaedia of Islam*, 2d ed.)

6. In addition to Jazīrī, see Mouradgea D'Ohsson, *Tableau général de l'empire othoman*, 7 vols. (Paris, 1788–1824), 4:76; Kâtib Çelebi, *The Balance of Truth*, trans. G. L. Lewis (London, George Allen and Unwin, 1957), p. 60; Edward William Lane, *An Account of the Manners and Customs of the Modern Egyptians*, 5th ed., ed. Stanley Poole (London, 1860; reprint, New York: Dover, 1973), pp. 332–33; Carsten Niebuhr, *Travels through Arabia and other Countries in the East*, trans. Robert Heron, 2 vols. (Edinburgh, 1792; reprint, Beirut, n.d.), 1:397–98; Muḥammad ibn Maḥmūd al-Zaynī al-Ḥusaynī, [*Risāla fī al-qahwa*], ms. Princeton, Yahuda coll. (catalogue Mach no. 2082), fol. 168r.

7. De Sacy's attribution of the name "Bā 'Alawī" to any sort of 'Alid descent is not necessarily the case here, since this could also be the large clan, without any such claim, of Yemen and the Ḥaḍramawt (see Oskar Löfgren, "Bā 'Alawī," in *The Encyclopaedia of Islam*, 2d ed.).

8. De Sacy assumes here that the word *al-ma'rūf* (known as) needs to be supplied in the text, that the name should be "Muḥammad (al-ma'rūf) bi-Afḍal al-Ḥaḍrimī." It is far more likely that there is no mistake in the mss., neither of which (ms. Paris 8v; ms. Escurial 11v) contains "al-ma'rūf," but rather that he was a member of the Bā Faḍl clan of the Ḥaḍramawt (see Maḥmūd Ghul, "Faḍl, Bā," in *The Encyclopaedia of Islam*, 2d ed.). It is perhaps worthy of note that one of the *nisbas* traditionally associated with the Bā-Faḍl clan is given as Madhḥij, to which one of the *nisbas* given in Sakhāwī for al-Dhabḥānī also refers.

9. See Jazīrī, *'Umdat al-ṣafwa*, ed. de Sacy, 1:142–45; ms. Paris, fols. 7v–8v; ms. Escurial, fols. 10r–11r.

10. Ibn al-'Imād, for instance, has nothing about him. Abū Makhrama (*Tārīkh thaghr 'Adan*, ed. Oskar Löfgren, 2 vols. [Uppsala: Almquist and Wiksells, 1939–50], 2:219) does mention a Muḥammad ibn Sa'īd al-Madhḥijī, a Shāfi'ī and a member of the Qādirī order, but has no other information on the man, not even the dates of his birth and death.

11. *Al-Ḍaw' al-lāmi' li-ahl al-qarn al-tāsi'*, 12 vols. (Cairo, 1934–36; reprint, Beirut, 1966), 7:249–50.

12. Kâtib Çelebi, *Balance of Truth*, p. 60.

13. See Franz Rosenthal, *The Herb* (Leiden: E. J. Brill, 1971), p. 65, where he discusses the vocabulary evidence concerning the smoking or eating of hashish.

14. See C. van Arendonk, "Ḳahwa," in *The Encyclopaedia of Islam*, 2d ed.

15. D'Ohsson, *Tableau général*, 4:76.

16. Fakhr al-Dīn al-Makkī was the author of *Ithārat al-nakhwa bi-ḥill al-qahwa*, often cited by Jazīrī (*'Umdat al-ṣafwa*, ed. de Sacy, 1:140; ms. Paris, fol. 5v; ms. Escurial, fol. 6v). There is no mention of the work in Brockelmann, *Geschichte der arabischen Literatur*, 2 vols. with 3 supplementary vols. (Leiden: E. J. Brill, 1937–49) (hereafter cited as *GAL*).

17. The phrase *sayyidunā* (our master) appears in ms. Escurial (fol. 12r) but not in ms. Paris or ed. de Sacy.

18. "Fa-imtaḥanūhā fa-wajadūhā ta'malu 'amalahu." De Sacy (1:143) believes that the suffix on " 'amalahu" refers to the word *bunn*, that the *qahwa* made of the *bunn* had the same effect as the *bunn* itself, reasoning that the suffix probably does not refer to *qāt*, which is too far removed, or to *kafta*, which is feminine. This is possible, since many were known to chew the beans and not make coffee out of them. But the expression that follows, "with little expense or trouble," suggests a comparison with something else, but with what? With *bunn*? Not likely, since its expense would be the same, and one had to go to the added trouble of brewing it. I believe that it refers to *qāt*, that the *qahwa* made of *bunn* does the same job as that made from *qāt*, but with little expense or trouble.

19. Jazīrī, *'Umdat al-ṣafwa*, ed. de Sacy, 1:145–46; ms. Paris, fols. 8v–9r; ms. Escurial, fols. 11v–12r.

20. "Al-qahwa: al-khamr; summiyat bi-dhālika li-anna tuqhī shāribahā 'an al-ṭa'ām ayy tadhhaba bi-shahwatihi" (Ibn Manẓūr, *Lisān al-'arab* [Beirut, 1955], s.v. "qahwa").

21. Jazīrī, *'Umdat al-ṣafwa*, ed. de Sacy, 1:140; ms. Paris, fol. 5v; ms. Escurial, fols. 6v–7r.

22. Jazīrī (*'Umdat al-ṣafwa*, ed. de Sacy, 1:141) notes that some of the Sufis originally called coffee *qihwa*, with a *kasra* (short "i"), to distinguish it from wine.

23. See the Chevalier d'Arvieux, as quoted by Philippe Sylvestre Dufour in his *Traitez nouveau et curieux du Café, du Thé, et du Chocolate* (Lyon, 1685), pp. 21–22.

24. Niebuhr, *Travels*, 1:397–99. Niebuhr also seemed to believe that the man was held as a patron saint of coffee drinkers throughout the Muslim world.

25. Van Arendonk ("Ḳahwa," in *The Encyclopaedia of Islam*, 2d ed.), on the authority of al-Sharjī, gives 1418 (A.H. 814) as the date of al-Shādhilī's death, although the account does not make it entirely clear that we are speaking of the same person. Van Arendonk, who originally wrote the article for the first edition of *The Encyclopaedia of Islam*, depended heavily on the *Ṣafwat al-ṣafwa fī bayān ḥukm al-qahwa* of ibn al-'Aydarūs, ms. Berlin (cat. Ahlwardt no. 5479). This, unfortunately, can no longer be found at the Staatsbibliothek.

26. Najm al-Dīn al-Ghazzī, *al-Kawākib al-sā'ira bi-a'yān al-mi'a al-'āshira*, ed. Jibrā'īl Jabbūr, 3 vols. (Beirut: American University of Beirut, 1945–58), 1:114.

27. "'Alā 'ādat al-ṣāliḥīn." I have translated *ṣāliḥ* as "pious," although it seems to have a meaning more specific to Sufism, along the lines of: one who is well known for his piety and devotion to the Way.

28. For a short time Ibn Maylaq was *qāḍī al-quḍāt* under Barqūq. See Brockelmann, *GAL*, 2:119–20. "Ibn Mablaq" in *Kawākib* is certainly a misprint.

29. See D. S. Margoliouth, "Shādhilīya" in *The Encyclopaedia of Islam*.

30. Perhaps the most dramatic and well known of these motions is the "whirling" dance of the dervishes of the Mevlevi order.

31. Rosenthal, *The Herb*, p. 71.

32. He tells us, for instance, of his frequent visits to and private audiences with one of the leading Sufis of Mecca, who was also a Mālikī *qāḍī* (see Jazīrī, *'Umdat al-ṣafwa*, ed. de Sacy, 1:141–42).

33. Jazīrī, *'Umdat al-ṣafwa*, ms. Paris, fols. 2r–2v; ms. Escurial, fol. 2v; not in ed. de Sacy.

34. Jazīrī, *'Umdat al-ṣafwa*, ed. de Sacy, 1:147.

35. Ibid., 1:146–47.

36. Ibid., 1:147–48.

37. See quotation below, chapter 6, p. 74.

CHAPTER THREE

1. Jazīrī, *'Umdat al-ṣafwa*, ed. de Sacy, 1:148.

2. We must not, however, be misled by the existence of a manuscript (Berlin, cat. Ahlwardt no. 5476) attributed to Suyūṭī,

who died in 1505 (A.H. 911). Internal evidence (see Appendix) makes it clear that he could not, indeed, have been the author of the work.

3. See for example, the works of al-Fākihī (d. 1538 [A.H. 945]) and al-Nahrawālī (d. 1582 [A.H. 990]), both in Ferdinand Wüstenfeld, *Die Chroniken der Stadt Mekka*, 4 vols. (Leipzig, 1857–61; reprint, Beirut, 1964), vols. 2 and 3 respectively.

4. Brockelmann, *GAL*, 2:387.

5. Jazīrī, *'Umdat al-ṣafwa*, ed. de Sacy, 1:152–53. Jazīrī mentions these visits to point out the later approval of coffee by Meccan jurists. This Sa'd al-Dīn ibn al-'Arrāq, he tells us, was a great coffee drinker, who served it regularly to Jazīrī when the latter came to Mecca.

6. A position of uncertain responsibility: Reinhart Dozy refers the reader to de Sacy's edition and translation of this very text for his definition "lieutenant" (*Supplément aux dictionnaires arabes* [Leiden: E. J. Brill, 1967]).

7. Khā'ir Beg's governorship, but nothing concerning this incident, is mentioned by Ibn Zuhayr, *Kitāb al-Jāmi' al-laṭīf* and al-Nahrawālī, *Kitāb al-A'lām* . . . , in Wüstenfeld, *Mekka*, 2:339 and 3:338 respectively. The position of *muḥtasib* included duty as inspector of markets and overseer of public morality (see Glossary).

8. Jazīrī, *'Umdat al-ṣafwa*, ed. de Sacy, 1:158.

9. "'Alā hai'a al-sharaba alladhīn yata'āṭūna al-muskir." Jazīrī, *'Umdat al-ṣafwa*, ed. de Sacy, 1:158.

10. Ibid., 1:158–60.

11. In spite of their considerable reputations (they were the personal physicians to a number of the lofty of Mecca, including two of the sharīfs of the town), Jazīrī has only lukewarm respect for their abilities. He says that they were skilled in logic and speculative philosophy, with some abilities in medicine, but that they claimed a rank in legal studies that was not really theirs.

12. Jazīrī, *'Umdat al-ṣafwa*, ed. de Sacy, 1:164.

13. "Fa-in kāna yuḥṣalu min maṭbūkh qishrihi ḍarar fī al-badn aw fī al-'aql aw yuḥṣalu bihi nashwa wa-ladhdha wa-ṭarab fa-innahu ḥarām" (Jazīrī, *'Umdat al-ṣafwa*, ed. de Sacy, 1:161).

14. Probably the *Minhāj al-bayān fī mā yasta'miluhu al-insān*, by Abū 'Alī Yaḥyā ibn 'Isā ibn Jazla (d. 1100 [A.H. 493]), a handbook on simple and compound medicaments. See Brockelmann, *GAL*, 1:485; *Supplement*, 1:888.

15. Jazīrī, *'Umdat al-ṣafwa*, ms. Paris, fol. 18v; ms. Escurial, fols. 23v–24r; not in ed. de Sacy.

16. Ghazzī (*Kawākib*, 1:18) gives the date and place of his death as Muḥarram 919 (A.D. 1513) at ʻAqaba.

17. Brockelmann (*GAL*, *Supplement*, 2:142) places their death during the conquest in 1517 (A.H. 923) (1512 is a misprint).

18. See Jazīrī, *ʻUmdat al-ṣafwa*, ed. de Sacy 1:151–52; ms. Paris, fol. 11r; ms. Escurial, fol. 15r.

19. Ibn al-ʻImād, *Shadharāt al-dhahab*, 8:196–99, has a long entry on his career.

20. While it is entirely possible that even at this early date coffeehouses and the coffee trade were used as a cover for the sale of entirely different kinds of pleasure, as discussed in chapter seven, the text here seems to make no allusion at all to such a situation.

21. It is not only from Jazīrī that we have his reputation as a partisan of coffee. Ibn al-ʻImād (*Shadharāt al-dhahab*, 8:337–38) and Ghazzī (*Kawākib*, 2:198) tell us that while Saʻd al-Dīn lived in Damascus he not only drank coffee, but countenanced the operation of the coffee shops which proliferated there—a policy quite obviously contrary to that of his father's toward these institutions.

22. The date roughly corresponds to when Kâtib Çelebi (*Balance of Truth*, p. 60) reports the introduction of coffee by ship to Asia Minor, though its sale in shops in Istanbul was still some eleven years off. This early decree against coffee was exceptional: in general, the attitude of the Ottoman government toward coffee was to remain favorable for several decades.

23. It is hardly likely that a "Greek," as the original reads, would have lived at Mecca ("Dhukira anna sabab dhālika shakwa imra'a rūmīya kānat mujāwira bi-Makka qabla dhālika"). It is therefore best to assume that "rūmīya" here means a Turk from Anatolia, or perhaps Istanbul.

24. On Sunbāṭī's life, see Ghazzī, *Kawākib*, 1:221–23; Ibn al-ʻImād, *Shadharāt al-dhahab*, 8:179.

25. Jazīrī, *ʻUmdat al-ṣafwa*, ms. Paris, fol. 20v; ms. Escurial, fol. 26v.

26. See Ghazzī, *Kawākib*, 2:111; Ibn al-ʻImād, *Shadharāt al-dhahab*, 8:280–81.

27. Muḥyi al-Dīn Muḥammad ibn Ilyās (d. 1547), a Ḥanafī jurist, is referred to in the *ʻUmdat al-ṣafwa* as *qāḍī Miṣr* (judge of Cairo). Ibn al-ʻImād (*Shadharāt al-dhahab*, 8:303) says he became *a* judge in Cairo (*ṣāra qāḍiy*[an] *bi-Miṣr*). Also see Ghazzī (*Kawākib*, 2:28–29), and Brockelmann (*GAL*, *Supplement* 2:642) on his career, which included the *kadı askerlik*s of both Anatolia and Rumelia, and

a stint as a mufti in Istanbul. His assignment to Cairo came rather early in his career, immediately after he had lived in Bursa. Since he was apparently new to Egypt, it is hardly surprising that he had to seek the advice of others concerning coffee.

28. For a full account of this incident, see Jazīrī, *'Umdat al-ṣafwa*, ed. de Sacy, 1:154.

29. Cf., for example, Maqrīzī, *al-Sulūk li-ma'rifat duwal al-mulūk*, ed. M. M. Ziyāda, 2 vols. (Cairo, 1936–58), 1:373, 525, 553, 578, 595, 865, 941.

CHAPTER FOUR

1. Abū Bakr Muḥammad al-Sarakhsī, *al-Mabsūṭ*, 30 vols. (Cairo, 1324–31/1906–12), 24:2. Western scholars generally seek the source of this gradual evolution in Muḥammad's changing problems in administering the community, particularly in dealing with civil strife within the community, especially that between the natives of Medina and the Meccan "emigrants."

2. Georg Jacob, *Altarabisches Beduinenleben*, 2d ed. (Berlin: Mayer and Müller, 1897), p. 96.

3. Jacob, *Altarabisches Beduinenleben*, p. 97; Ignazio Guidi, *L'Arabie antéislamique* (Paris: Paul Geuthner, 1921), p. 55; W. Montgomery Watt, *Muḥammad at Medina* (Oxford: Oxford University Press, 1956), p. 299. Date wines fell into two categories: (*a*) those made from fresh, ripe, juicy dates (*ruṭab*) from which the juice was pressed and allowed to ferment, producing a beverage called *sakar*; (*b*) the infusion (*naqī'*) of dried dates (*tamr*) in water, that is allowed to ferment, known as *faḍīkh*. In legal discussions, however, all fermented date beverages are usually included under the rubric *sakar*, or are simply called *nabīdh al-tamr*.

4. I have chosen to translate *ithm* here as "harm," in opposition to "benefit." The word is one charged with a variety of meanings, though not mutually exclusive ones. Ibn Qutayba (*al-Ashriba*, ed. Muḥammad Kurd 'Alī [Damascus, 1366/1947], p. 65), in discussing the arguments of those who point out certain benefits of wine, mentions the use of *ithm* as meaning "punishment": "fa-al-ithm al-'adhāb wa-ka-dhālika al-āthām qāla 'wa-man yaf'alu dhālika yalqā āthām^{an}' [Qur'ān 25:68] ayy 'aqāb^{an}." Sarakhsī sees *ithm* in the more traditional light of "sin" (*Mabsūṭ*, 24:3), quoting Qur'ān 7:33, where *ithm* is included with "abominations" (*fawāḥish*), "rebellion" (*baghya*), "giving partners to God" (*shirk*) and "saying about God

what you do not know." By extension, one might say that *ithm* is a sin that leads to final retribution. Sarakhsī also cites a verse where *ithm* is used as one of the words for wine.

5. Sarakhsī, *Mabsūṭ*, 24:2–3; al-Kāsānī, *Badā'i' al-ṣanā'i' fī tartīb al-sharā'i'*, 7 vols. (Cairo, 1328/1910), 5:112; Burhān al-Dīn al-Marghīnānī, *al-Hidāya*, 4 vols. (Cairo, 1326/[1908–9]), 4:86–87; Ibn Nujaym, *al-Baḥr al-rā'iq sharḥ Kanz al-daqā'iq*, 8 vols. (Cairo, 1311/[1894]), 8:247; Mūllā Khusraw, *Durar al-ḥukkām fī sharḥ Ghurar al-aḥkām*, 2 vols. ([Istanbul], 1260/1844), 2:407; Ibrāhīm al-Ḥalabī, *Multaqā al-abḥur* (Būlāq, 1265/1848–49), pp. 347–49. A phrase, used by the Ḥanafīs in particular to discuss *khamr*, is that the prohibition is "clear-cut": *qaṭ'ī* or *maqṭū'*. See, among others, Kāsānī, *Badā'i' al-ṣanā'i'*, 5:115.

6. Ibn Qutayba, *Ashriba*, p. 17.

7. This attitude was not merely the province of "speculative philosophers." It calls to mind the story related by Ignaz Goldziher in which an Arab convert to Islam, who nonetheless remains very "old school" and attached to traditional values, continues to drink wine, saying "'but I have not found that wine is forbidden. It is only written: Will you abstain from it? ... and we both replied to that question No, and God was silent and we were silent too.'" (*Muslim Studies*, ed. S. M. Stern, trans. C. R. Barber and S. M. Stern, 2 vols. [London: George Allen and Unwin, 1967–71], 1:32).

8. Sarakhsī (*Mabsūṭ*, 24:3), setting aside for the moment that it was forbidden in and of itself, argues with them that unlike other foods, the desire to consume wine increases proportionally with the amount already drunk. With other foods one reaches satiety; with wine, the more one drinks, the more one wishes to drink.

9. Sarakhsī, *Mabsūṭ*, 24:3; Kāsānī, *Badā'i' al-ṣanā'i'*, 5:113; Ibn Nujaym, *al-Baḥr al-rā'iq*, 8:247; Mūllā Khusraw, *Durar al-ḥukkām*, p. 408; Ḥalabī, *Multaqā al-abḥur*, p. 348; Marghīnānī, *Hidāya*, 4:87.

10. Sarakhsī, *Mabsūṭ*, 24:28–29. Even in the case of dire need because of thirst, the Shāfi'īs would not allow its consumption. The Ḥanbalīs would allow it in case of extreme emergency, such as choking, but even then polluted water or urine were to be used instead if they were available. See Manṣūr ibn Yūnus al-Bahūtī, *al-Rawḍ al-murbi' bi-sharḥ Zād al-mustaqni'–Mukhtaṣar al-muqni'* (Cairo, 1380/-1960–61), p. 348.

11. For the essentials of each school's beverage laws, see: for the Shāfi'ī school: Ibn Qāsim al-Ghazzī, *Fatḥ al-qarīb* (commentary on *al-Taqrīb* of Abū Shujā'), trans. L. W. C. van den Berg, *La révélation*

de l'Omniprésent (Leiden: E. J. Brill, 1894), pp. 578–81.; Abū Isḥāq Ibrāhīm al-Shīrāzī, *al-Tanbīh fī al-fiqh 'alā madhhab al-Imām al-Shāfi'ī* (Cairo, 1370/1951), p. 151; Shams al-Dīn Muḥammad al-Ramlī, *Nihāyat al-muḥtāj ilā sharḥ al-Minhāj*, 8 vols. (Cairo, [1357/1938]), 8:9–10; Ibn Ḥajar al-Haythamī, *Tuḥfat al-muḥtāj bi-sharḥ al-Minhāj*, 10 vols. (Cairo, [1315/1898]), 9:166–67; for the Mālikī school: al-Qayrawānī, *Risāla* (Cairo, [1930]), p. 122, trans. Léon Bercher (*La Risâla*), 3rd ed. (Algiers, 1949), p. 299; Khalīl ibn Isḥāq, *al-Mukhtaṣar* (Paris, 1318/1900), p. 235, trans. G. -H. Bousquet, *Abrégé de la loi musulmane selon le rite de l'imâm Mâlek*, Bibliothèque de la faculté de droit et des sciences économiques d'Alger, vol. 40 (Algiers and Paris, 1962), 4:57; for the Ḥanbalī school: 'Umar ibn al-Ḥusayn al-Khiraqī, *al-Mukhtaṣar* ([Damascus], 1379/[1959–60]), p. 196; Mūsā ibn Aḥmad al-Ḥujāwī, *al-Iqnā' fī fiqh al-Imām Aḥmad ibn Ḥanbal*, 4 vols. (Cairo, [1351/1932]), 4:266; Ibn Qudāma, *Le précis de droit d'Ibn Qudāma ...*, trans. Henri Laoust (Beirut, 1950), pp. 222, 265; Bahūtī, *al-Rawḍ al-murbi'*, p. 348.

12. See, among others, al-Qudūrī, *Matn al-Qudūrī fī al-fiqh* [*al-Mukhtaṣar*] (Cairo, 1377/1957), p. 98; Ḥalabī, *Multaqā al-abḥur*, pp. 347–49. Not only is this latter among the more concise books of *furū'*, but for our purposes one of the most important, since it was a standard part of the curriculum for legal training in the Ottoman state.

13. The last two beverages are examples of the general category known as *nabīdhs*. These were generally infusions (*naqī'*) of fruits, grains or other material (such as honey) in water that were allowed to ferment. In his *Social Life under the 'Abbāsids* (London: Longmans, 1979, p. 110), M. M. Ahsan mentions that there was some debate over whether *nabīdh* was alcoholic or not, and from the context of his remarks he suggests that nonalcoholic drinks called *nabīdhs* were served at meals. Be that as it may, Ibn Qutayba (*Ashriba*, pp. 20–21) believes firmly that the term is to be applied only to alcoholic beverages, and the context in which the word is used in works of practical jurisprudence would tend to bear this out.

14. Among the scholars favoring such an interpretation are: Qayrawānī, *Risāla*, p. 122 (Bercher, *La Risâla*, p. 299); Bahūtī, *al-Rawḍ al-murbī'*, p. 348; Ḥujāwī, *Iqnā'*, 4:266. Ibn Qutayba (*Ashriba*, p. 99) also advocates this stand.

15. See Sarakhsī, *Mabsūṭ*, 24:4–5; Ibn Nujaym, *al-Baḥr al-rā'iq*, 8:247; Mūllā Khusraw, *Durar al-ḥukkām*, p. 407; Marghīnānī, *Hidā-*

ya, 4:86; ʿAbd al-Raḥmān Shaykh-zāde, *Majmaʿ al-anhur fī sharḥ Multaqā al-abḥur*, 2 vols. (Istanbul, 1276/[1859]), 2:815.

16. A *frq* is a measure of uncertain size. Ibn Qutayba, in discussing this *ḥadīth*, reminds the reader that one must use common sense in determining what is meant. The *farq*, as it was known to the common people, was a measure of 120 *raṭls*, an amount that would seem impossible to drink, and thus difficult to base any sort of prohibition on. He prefers to read *faraq*, which he says is a measure of 16 *raṭls*. *Ashriba*, pp. 109–10.

17. Sarakhsī, *Mabsūṭ*, 24:17.

18. Ibn Qutayba, *Ashriba*, pp. 38, 46–48. Sarakhsī (*Mabsūṭ*, 24:16) reports that during the pilgrimage, Muḥammad asked for drink and was given this *nabīdh*, but when he brought it near his mouth he scowled and gave it back. When al-ʿAbbās asked him if it was forbidden, Muḥammad took it back and cut it with water, then drank. Sarakhsī maintains that he scowled because it was strong, not, as some claimed, because it was sour. Edward Lane (*An Arabic-English Lexicon* [London, 1863–93], p. 1386) defines *siqāya* as: "A place for giving drink or watering ... a place in which beverage is made, or prepared, at the fairs, or festivals, etc.: and particularly a place in which a beverage made of raisins steeped in water was given at the general assembly of the pilgrims ... and *siqāyat al-ḥajj* means the beverage made of raisins steeped in water which the tribe of Ḳureysh used to give to pilgrims to drink: it was under the superintendence of El-Abbás in the Time of Ignorance and in El-Islám."

19. Sarakhsī, *Mabsūṭ*, 24:5.

20. "Kull muskir khamr wa-kull muskir ḥarām." See Ibn Qutayba, *Ashriba*, pp. 22–23, 101–2; Sarakhsī, *Mabsūṭ*, 24:15–16 (where he attributes these arguments to al-Shāfiʿī and Mālik); Bahūtī, *al-Rawḍ al-murbīʿ*, p. 348.

21. They do, however, make one concession to redefinition of *khamr* by *ḥadīth*: they regard as valid and binding the reported statement of Muḥammad, "*Khamr* [comes] from two plants, the vine and the [date] palm" (al-khamr min hātayn sajaratayn al-karm wa-al-nakhl). See Sarakhsī, *Mabsūṭ*, 24:3–4; Kāsānī, *Badāʾiʿ al-ṣanāʾiʿ*, 5:114–15; Ibn Nujaym, *al-Baḥr al-rāʾiq*, 8:248; Marghīnānī, *Hidāya*, 4:87.

22. "Ḥurrimat al-khamr li-ʿaynihā wa-al-muskir min kull sharāb" (Ibn Qutayba, *Ashriba*, p. 45; Sarakhsī, *Mabsūṭ*, 24:8–9; Kāsānī,

Badā'i' al-ṣanā'i', 5:112, 115). This is variously attributed to Muḥammad himself or to Ibn 'Abbās.

23. Sarakhsī, *Mabsūṭ*, 24:8–9.

24. Actually, there is one way for the substance to become licit—by becoming vinegar (*takhlīl*).

25. Sarakhsī, *Mabsūṭ*, 24:18; Kāsānī, *Badā'i' al-ṣanā'i'*, 5:113; Ibn Nujaym, *al-Baḥr al-rā'iq*, 8:249. Both Ibn Nujaym (8:247) and Marghīnānī (*Hidāya*, 4:86–87) clarify the essential nature of the prohibition, saying that the proscription of *khamr* is in no way linked to drunkenness (*sukr*), unlike the prohibition of other drinks. The Qur'ān calls it an abomination (*rijs*), and an abomination is forbidden by its very essence.

26. Qudūrī, *Mukhtaṣar*, p. 98; Sarakhsī, *Mabsūṭ*, 24:17; Ibn Nujaym, *al-Baḥr al-rā'iq*, 8:248; Mūllā Khusraw, *Durar al-ḥukkām*, p. 408; Shaykh-zāde, *Majma' al-anhur*, 2:816.

27. Ibn Qutayba, *Ashriba*, p. 53.

28. Mālik: "Al-sakrān alladhī yaghību wa-yakhliṭu"; Shāfi'ī: "Al-sakrān alladhī fāraqa mā kāna 'alayhi min al-ḥilm wa-al-sukūn ilā al-safah wa-al-jahl" (both quoted by Ibn Qutayba, *Ashriba*, pp. 100–101); Abū Ḥanīfa: "Al-sakrān alladhī yadhhabu 'aqluhu fa-lā ya'rifu qalīl^{an} wa-lā kathīr^{an}" (Ibn Qutayba, *Ashriba*, pp. 100–101); Ibn Nujaym: "Al-sakrān alladhī yuḥaddu huwa alladhī lā ya'qulu muṭlaq^{an} qalīl^{an} kāna aw kathīr^{an} wa-lā ya'rifu al-rajul min al-mar'a wa-lā al-arḍ min al-samā'" (*al-Baḥr al-rā'iq*, 8:249); Mūllā Khusraw: "Al-sukr ḥāla ta'riḍu lil-insān min imtilā' dimāghihi min al-abkhira al-mutaṣā'ida ilayhi fa-yata'aṭṭlu 'aqluhu al-mumayyiz bayna al-umūr al-ḥasana wa-al-qabīḥa" (*Durar al-ḥukkām*, p. 409).

29. Quoted in Jazīrī, *'Umdat al-ṣafwa*, ms. Paris, fol. 27r; ms. Escurial, fol. 34r.

30. Jazīrī, *'Umdat al-ṣafwa*, ms. Escurial, fol. 8r.

31. A narcotic of uncertain origin, sometimes likened to hashish.

32. *Risāla fī aḥkām al-qahwa*, ms. Berlin, cat. Ahlwardt no. 5476, fol. 11r. On the authorship of this ms., see Appendix.

33. See Jazīrī, *'Umdat al-ṣafwa*, ms. Paris, fol. 28v; ms. Escurial, fols. 35v–36r.

34. *Iṣṭifā' al-ṣafwa li-taṣfiyat al-qahwa*, ms. Leiden, cat. de Jong and de Goeje no. 1872 (cod. 1138 Warn.), fols. 14r–14v (see Appendix).

35. See Jazīrī, *'Umdat al-ṣafwa*, ms. Paris, fol. 30v; ms. Escurial, fol. 38v.

36. Jazīrī, *'Umdat al-ṣafwa*, ms. Paris, fol. 30v; ms Escurial, fol. 38v. The word also appears—again attributed to the ubiquitous Ibn 'Abd al-Ghaffār—throughout the *Risāla fī aḥkām al-qahwa*, ms. Berlin.

37. *Risāla fī aḥkām al-qahwa*, ms. Berlin, fols. 12v–13r.

CHAPTER FIVE

1. This is usually based on Qur'ān 2:29: "It is He who created for you all that is on the earth" (Khalaqa lakum mā fī al-arḍ jamī'[an]).

2. *Iṣṭifā' al-ṣafwa*, ms. Leiden, fols. 15r–15v.

3. Ibn al-Jazzār, *Qam' al-wāshīn fī dhamm al-barrāshīn*, ms. Leiden, cat. de Jong and de Goeje no. 1880 (cod. 814[12] Warn.), fol. 275r–275v. On dietary laws in general, see Maxime Rodinson, "Ghidhā'" in *The Encyclopaedia of Islam*, 2d ed. He cites al-Ghazālī (*Iḥyā'* [Cairo, 1352/1933], 2:83) as the source of this principle.

4. Jazīrī, *'Umdat al-ṣafwa*, ed. de Sacy, 1:161–62.

5. The sources differ regarding their skill and reliability, ranging from the lavish praise of the official version to Jazīrī's disgusted contempt, and ill-concealed glee over their painful demise some years later. See Jazīrī, *'Umdat al-ṣafwa*, ed. de Sacy, 1:149, 157–64

6. Zaynī, [*Risāla fī al-qahwa*], fols. 168r–69v.

7. See Manfred Ullmann, *Die Medizin im Islam* (Leiden and Cologne: E. J. Brill, 1970), pp. 97–99; E. G. Browne, *Arabian Medicine* (Cambridge: Cambridge University Press, 1921), pp. 116–20.

8. Browne, *Arabian Medicine*, p. 119.

9. Zaynī: "Fa-alfaytu qishrahā wa-bunnahā bārid[an] yābis[an] illā anna al-kayfīyatayn al-madhkūratayn fī al-qishr fī awākhir al-daraja al-ūlā wa-fī al-bunn fī awāsiṭ al-thāniya" [*Risāla fī al-qahwa*], fol. 168v.

10. Kâtib Çelebi, *Balance of Truth*, p. 61. Though not a physician himself, he seems to have been well acquainted with contemporary medical opinion.

11. See Ullmann, *Medizin*, p. 181.

12. Anṭākī: "Wa-huwa ḥārr fī al-ūlā yābis fī al-thāniya wa-qad shā'a barduhu wa-yabsuhu wa-laysa ka-dhālika li-annahu murr wa-kull murr ḥārr" (*Tadhkirat ūlī al-albāb wa-al-jāmi' li-al-'ajab al-'ujāb*, 3 vols. [Cairo, 1371/1952], 1:86). There was an edition and translation of the section "*bunn*" done by the seventeenth-century English orientalist Edward Pococke, entitled *The Nature of the drink Kauhi or*

Coffe, and the Berry of which it is made (Oxford, 1659), but owing to numerous mistakes of reading and translation it is entirely unreliable.

13. This directly contradicts what Bradley suggests the Arabs believed, since he said that in summer they used only the husks, and in winter the kernels, the former being of a colder, and the latter of a hotter nature. *Coffee*, pp. 18–19.

14. Jazīrī, *'Umdat al-ṣafwa*, ms. Paris, fol. 6r; ms. Escurial, fol. 7v. A similar opinion is expressed by the author of the *Iṣṭifā' al-ṣafwa*, fol. 3v.

15. Zaynī, [*Risāla fī al-qahwa*], fol. 168r.

16. Ibid., fol. 169r.

17. Jazīrī stresses that those who opposed coffee particularly favored the interpretation of its being cold and dry (*'Umdat al-ṣafwa*, 1:141). Apparently there was far more concern, and consequently basis for attack, for a melancholic condition than for a bilious one, which would suffer from a hot and dry food.

18. Kâtib Çelebi, *Balance of Truth*, p. 62.

19. "Wa-rubbamā afḍā ilā mālīkhūliyā" (Anṭākī, *Tadhkirat ūlī al-albāb*, 1:86).

20. Louis Lémery, *A Treatise on Foods* . . . , anonymous English translation (London, 1704), p. 317.

21. Zaynī: "Wajaba al-iḥtimā' minhā 'alā sawdāwīyīn, bal al-tajriba nabba'at bi-ḍurrihā li-al-ṣafrāwīyīn" [*Risāla fī al-qahwa*], fol. 169r.

22. Kâtib Çelebi, *Balance of Truth*, p. 62.

23. Anṭākī, *Tadhkirat ūlī al-albāb*, 1:86.

24. " . . . mentem movet et turbat" (Bacon, *Historia vitae et mortis* [London, 1824 and other eds.], 1:25).

25. Anṭākī, *Tadhkirat ūlī al-albāb*, 1:86.

26. "Wa-yaqṭa'u shahwat al-bāh" (Anṭākī, *Tadhkirat ūlī al-albāb*, 1:86).

27. See Lémery, *Foods*, pp. 317–18. John Chamberlayne (*The Natural History of Coffee, Thee, Chocolate, Tobacco* . . . [London, 1682], p. 5) relates a humorous Persian story, which he learned from the ambassador Olearius, of a king who, being addicted to coffee, lost interest in sexual relations with his queen. She, upon seeing men about to geld a stallion one day, told them in frustration that the same end might be effected by giving the beast coffee. Also see La Roque, *Arabie Heureuse*, pp. 265–66.

28. The author of the *Iṣṭifā' al-ṣafwa* (ms. Leiden, fol. 16v) maintained that coffee cured hemorrhoids. Lémery, whom I suspect of

having gotten much of his information on the medical properties of coffee from Anṭākī, or more probably from Pococke's little translation, does however contradict him on the matter of coffee causing headaches. He claims that it tends to relieve headaches (*Treatise on Foods*, p. 316). This may, however, be connected with one benefit of coffee frequently encountered in European sources, that it "suppresses the fumes caused by wine," i.e., it is good for regaining sobriety or treating a hangover. See, for example, Jean de Thévenot, *Voyages en Europe, Asie et Afrique*, 3rd ed., 2 vols. (Amsterdam, 1727), 1:103; [Audiger], *La maison réglée* . . . (Amsterdam, 1697), p. 297; Bradley, *Coffee*, pp. 19–21. It should offer little surprise that this is one benefit of coffee not mentioned at all in Muslim sources.

29. Dufour, *Traitez nouveaux*, pp. 33–35. He remarks, however, that the Turks do not always hold to this, but even considered coffee nourishing.

30. Zaynī, [*Risāla fī al-qahwa*], fols. 169v–70r.

31. In addition to the physicians whom I treat here at length, it is reported that Badr al-Dīn al-Kawsūnī, court physician to Süleyman I, approved of it. See Rodinson, "Ghidhā'."

32. Kâtib Çelebi, *Balance of Truth*, p. 61.

33. *Iṣṭifā' al-ṣafwa*, ms. Leiden, fols. 4v–5r.

34. Jazīrī, *'Umdat al-ṣafwa*, ed. de Sacy, 1:141.

35. The virtues of staying up at night for religious contemplation are stressed in the Qur'ān (17:59; 73:1–6 and elsewhere), a fact to which many advocates of coffee find reason to allude. *Iṣṭifā' al-ṣafwa*, ms. Leiden, fols. 7r–8r.

36. See for example, Bacon, *Historia vitae et mortis*, 1:25; Thévenot, *Voyages*, p. 103.

37. Walter Rumsey, *Organon Salutis. An Instrument to cleanse the Stomach, As also divers new Experiments of the virtue of Tobacco and Coffee: How much they conduce to preserve humane health* (London, 1657), preface. This is a strange little book, in which the author advocates the use of coffee and tobacco along with a whalebone stomach-stirrer of his own patent, to induce vomiting and thereby cleanse the stomach of "crudities," to which he attributes many of the ills of mankind. Leonhart Rauwolff also touts coffee's benefits for the digestive tract (*Aigentliche Beschreibung der Raiss inn die Morgenlaender* [1593; reprint, with introduction by Dietmar Henze, Graz, 1971], p. 102).

38. William Biddulph, in Samuel Purchas (1527–1626), *Hakluytus Posthumus or Purchas His Pilgrimes*, 20 vols. (Glasgow: James

MacLehose and Sons, 1905–7), 8:266; Bacon, *Natural History* (London, 1824), 8:738; Thévenot, *Voyages*, 1:103; Audiger, *Maison réglée*, p. 298; Bradley, *Coffee*, pp. 19–20.

39. On coffee, and the benefits of hot drinks in general, see also Ed. Jorden, *A Discourse of Naturall Bathes and Minerall Waters*, 3rd ed. (London, 1663), pp. 128–29.

40. *Risāla fī aḥkām al-qahwa*, ms. Berlin, fol. 11v.

41. Ibid., fols. 13r–13v.

CHAPTER SIX

1. André Raymond has much to say on the economic importance of coffee. See *Artisans et commerçants au Caire au XVIII siècle*, 2 vols. (Damascus, 1973), pp. 107, 121–28, 136–42.

2. Bradley, *Coffee*, p. 24.

3. Quoted in Jazīrī, *'Umdat al-ṣafwa*, ed. de Sacy, 1:148–49.

4. Dufour, *Traitez nouveaux*, p. 37.

5. Jazīrī, *'Umdat al-ṣafwa*, ed. de Sacy, 1:148.

6. Ibrāhīm Peçevi, *Tārīh-i Peçevi*, 2 vols. (Istanbul, 1281–83/1864–67), 1:363. This often cited passage has frequently been translated (see for example, Bernard Lewis, *Istanbul and the Civilization of the Ottoman Empire* [Norman, Oklahoma: University of Oklahoma Press, 1963], pp. 132–33).

7. Judging from the content and tone of what is said, it is not at all likely that he was told this by one of those whom he caught drinking. It is possible that one of his confederates gave him this information, but it is more likely that here the "yuqālu lahu" (he is told) formula is merely a device for introducing the polemics of the authors of the report themselves. One tends to agree with Jazīrī that much of the report, including the fact that Khā'ir Beg was entirely ignorant of the existence of such places until that night, betrays a bit of art directed toward the goal of discrediting the drink.

8. Jazīrī, *'Umdat al-ṣafwa*, ms. Paris, fol. 17r; ms. Escurial, fol. 22r. His source for such knowledge of events that took place long before he wrote is not clear; he probably had much of this chapter on what happened at Mecca from Ibn 'Abd al-Ghaffār and Fakhr al-Dīn al-Makkī.

9. We know, for instance, that Mamluk governments often rewarded retainers with the proceeds from the taxes on wine and taverns, a practice which, like the existence of taverns, is confirmed if only by the accounts of its abolition. Similarly, Ottoman cadestral

registers from the sixteenth century often list among the revenues going to the sultan or governor the tax on the wine-houses in the cities of Palestine. See Amnon Cohen and Bernard Lewis, *Population and Revenue in the Towns of Palestine in the Sixteenth Century* (Princeton: Princeton University Press, 1978), pp. 68, 152, 169. One finds similar taxes (as well as taxes on the "hashish house") in the registers for Syrian Tripoli from the same period. See R. Hattox, "Some Ottoman Tapu Defters for Tripoli in the Sixteenth Century," *al-Abhath* 29 (1981): 80–81.

10. See Ira Lapidus, *Muslim Cities in the Later Middle Ages*, Harvard Middle Eastern Studies no. 11 (Cambridge, Mass.: Harvard University Press, 1967), p. 82. Also see Franz Rosenthal, *Gambling in Islam* (Leiden: E. J. Brill, 1975), p. 156, where the gambler, a figure later to appear in the coffee shop, is also included among this unsavory crowd.

11. A contemporary equivalent, especially in the Turkish part of the empire, was the *bozahane* (see chapter eight).

12. See Raymond, *Artisans et commerçants*, p. 316; Lane, *Modern Egyptians*, p. 333.

13. Biddulph, in Purchas, *Hakluytus Posthumus*, 8:266.

14. Certainly there are larger ones, both on a grand scale and "medium" neighborhood cafés, often referred to now as *kıraathanes*, "reading houses." There are, however, still small stall-type shops, which can accommodate maybe fifteen customers, while the overflow is consigned to benches outside, no great treat in the more severe Istanbul winter.

15. Dufour, *Traitez nouveaux*, p. 37.

16. Jean de Thévenot, *Suite du voyage du Levant*, 3rd ed., 2 vols. (Amsterdam, 1727), 1:71.

17. Pedro Teixeira, *The Travels of Pedro Teixeira*, translated and annotated by William F. Sinclair, Hakluyt Society, 2d series no. 9 (London, 1902), p. 62.

18. D'Ohsson, *Tableau général*, 4:81.

19. Thévenot, *Voyages*, 1:105.

20. Cf., D'Ohsson, *Tableau général*, 4:79; Lane, *Modern Egyptians*, pp. 137–38. That the practice was not entirely unknown, however, can be seen from Anṭākī's warning about the insalubrious consequences of adding milk. *Tadhkirat ūlī al-albāb*, 1:86; cited above.

21. Dufour, *Traitez nouveaux*, p. 58. Lane (*Modern Egyptians*, pp. 138–39) gives an extended description of how one flavored coffee

with ambergris. It is unlikely, however, that this latter flavoring was much used in the beverage offered in the coffeehouses.

22. Jazīrī, *'Umdat al-ṣafwa*, ed. de Sacy, 1:138.

23. Ibid., ms. Paris, fol. 22v; ms. Escurial, fol. 29r.

24. C. F. Beckingham, "Some Early Travels in Arabia," *Journal of the Royal Asiatic Society* (1949): 174.

25. La Roque, *Arabie Heureuse*, pp. 243–44.

26. Lane, *Modern Egyptians*, p. 333.

27. Niebuhr, *Travels*, 2:228–29.

28. Biddulph, in Purchas, *Hakluytus Posthumus*, 8:266.

29. Lane, *Modern Egyptians*, pp. 137, 333.

30. For example, Biddulph, in Purchas, *Hakluytus Posthumus*, 8:266.

31. Joannes Cotovicus [Johannes van Cootwijk], *Itinerarium hierosolymitanum et syriacum* (Antwerp, 1619), p. 484.

32. See Raymond, *Artisans et commerçants*, pp. 232–33.

33. Thévenot, *Voyages*, 1:104.

34. Jazīrī, *'Umdat al-ṣafwa*, ed. de Sacy, 1:148, 160.

35. Dufour, *Traitez nouveaux*, p. 57.

36. "Auß jrdinen unnd *Porcellanischen* tieffen Schälein" (Rauwolff, *Raiss inn die Morgenlaender*, p. 103).

37. Jazīrī, *'Umdat al-ṣafwa*, ms. Paris, fol. 17v; ms. Escurial, fols. 22v–23r. See also Lane, *Modern Egyptians*, pp. 137–38; Thévenot, *Voyages*, 1:102–3; Sandys, in Purchas, *Hakluytus Posthumus*, 8:146; Teixeira, *Travels*, p. 62.

38. "Thumma yaṣfū wa-yafturu" (Jazīrī, *'Umdat al-ṣafwa*, ms. Paris, fol. 22v); ms. Escurial, fol. 29r; see also Dufour, *Traitez nouveaux*, p. 63.

39. Thévenot, *Voyages*, 1:103.

40. Rauwolff tells us that they drink it "so warm alß sies könden erleiden" (*Raiss inn die Morgenlaender*, p. 103). See Biddulph, in Purchas, *Hakluytus Posthumus*, 8:266; Sandys, in *Hakluytus Posthumus*, 8:146–47; Teixeira, *Travels*, p. 62; Cotovicus, *Itinerarium*, p. 484. Thévenot (*Voyages*, 1:103) says that they have to be very careful to sip it slowly, for fear of being burned.

41. This is in sharp distinction to what one sees in places in the Mediterranean where the coffee is clear and without sediment. A Milanese being served a small cup of exquisite Italian coffee, hot out of the espresso machine, would be far more inclined to toss it all back in a matter of seconds.

42. Lane, *Modern Egyptians*, p. 507.

43. Cf., Jean Leclant, "Coffee and Cafés in Paris," in *Annales, E.S.C.* 6 (January-March 1951): 1–12; trans. Patricia M. Ranum in *Food and Drink in History, Selections from the "Annales,"* ed. Robert Forster and Orest Ranum (Baltimore and London: Johns Hopkins University Press, 1979), p. 89.

44. Sandys, in Purchas, *Hakluytus Posthumus*, 8:108.

CHAPTER SEVEN

1. Lane, *Modern Egyptians*, pp. 333, 474–75; Alexander Russell, *The Natural History of Aleppo* (London, 1756), p. 91; Kâtib Çelebi, *Balance of Truth*, p. 61; Dufour, *Traitez nouveaux*, p. 37; D'Ohsson, *Tableau général*, 4:78, 81.

2. "Relazione del Bailo Gianfrancesco Morosini (1585)" in *Le Relazioni degli Ambasciatori Veneti al Senato durante il Secolo Decimosesto*, ed. Eugenio Albèri, series 3, vol. 3 (Florence, 1855), pp. 267–68.

3. Teixeira, *Travels*, p. 62.

4. Thévenot, *Voyages*, 1:105.

5. "In the first day of our journey [to Bayt al-Faqīh], we traveled a parched and barren tract of country, along an arm of the sea, which penetrates a considerable way into the land. We rested in a coffee-shop situated near a village. *Mokeya* is the name given by Arabs to such coffee-houses which stand in the open country, and are intended, like our inns, for the accommodation of travellers. They are mere huts, and are scarcely furnished with a *Serir*, or a long seat of straw ropes; nor do they afford any refreshment but *Kischer*, a hot infusion of coffee-beans. This drink is served out in coarse earthenware cups; but persons of distinction carry always porcelain cups in their baggage. Fresh water is distributed *gratis*. The master of the coffee-house lives commonly in some neighboring village, whence he comes every day to wait for passengers" (Niebuhr, *Travels*, 1:265–66).

6. See Raymond, *Artisans et commerçants*, p. 262, for the eighteenth century. Even at the end of the sixteenth century this had already become the practice (see Muḥammad ibn ʿAbd al-Muʿṭī al-Isḥāqī, *Akhbār al-uwal fī man taṣarrafa fī Miṣr min arbāb al-duwal* [Cairo, 1311/1893–94], pp. 163, 174).

7. Raymond, *Artisans et commerçants*, p. 326.

8. For these and other descriptions, see Thévenot, *Suite du voyage*, 1:71–72.

9. The survey of Istanbul by one Zakarya Efendi in 1585–86 (A.H. 994) mentions the improbably high figure of 2,352 coffeehouses, not to mention 4,558 taverns (see Isḥāqī, *Akhbār al-uwal*, p. 146). Obviously, if even a fraction of this figure is accurate, the majority must have been built along modest lines. We can regard in the same light the count of two to three thousand coffee shops in Cairo in the early seventeenth century (cited in La Roque, *Arabie Heureuse*, p. 258).

10. Raymond tells of clusters of cafés near the Bab al-Naṣr along the Khalīj and near the citadel (*Artisans et commerçants*, p. 316).

11. Perhaps this indeed explains why some, like Peçevi, who have little hostility toward the coffeehouse, vigorously attack similar vices imported from the outside, like the use of tobacco.

12. Raymond, *Artisans et commerçants*, pp. 284–85, 290.

13. Ibid., pp. 427–28.

14. Isḥāqī, *Akhbār al-uwal*, p. 163.

15. Niebuhr, *Travels*, 2:264–66.

16. See Jean Leclant, "Coffee and Cafés," pp. 88–89.

17. Peçevi, *Tārīh*, 1:362.

18. Thévenot, *Voyages*, 1:105.

19. Andreas Tietze, trans. and ed., *Muṣṭafā 'Alī's Description of Cairo of 1599*, Österreichische Akademie der Wissenshaften philosophisch-historische Klasse Denkschriften, vol. 120 (Vienna, 1975), p. 53.

20. In spite of early reports to the contrary, women seldom are mentioned in our sources as coming to the coffeehouse. Their movements and expeditions outside the house were far more limited by social convention. Nonetheless a few structured activities allowed women relatively free association among themselves, particularly excursions to visit tombs, and scheduled trips to the bath-house. See, among others, Russell, *Aleppo*, p. 67, and Niebuhr, *Travels*, 1:60. The bath-house in particular seems to have served a function in female society similar to that of the coffeehouse among males. Sandys (in Purchas, *Hakluytus Posthumus*, 8:150–51), suggesting such a rôle for the bath, also implies that it served the same ends of debauchery and homosexual liaison among women that the café was suggested, by its more zealous detractors, to have had among males.

21. Dufour, *Traitez nouveaux*, p. 38; Biddulph, in Purchas, *Hakluytus Posthumus*, 8:266.

22. "Wa-khalaṭū al-jidd min al-dhikr bi-al-hazl min al-qawl wa-al-akdhāb" (Jazīrī, *'Umdat al-ṣafwa*, ms. Paris, fol. 2v; ms. Escurial,

fol. 2v). *Hazl*, in legal parlance, usually is given as the antonym of *jidd*, "seriousness"; it appears in the Qur'ān once (86:14), as an adjective describing what the Qur'ān is not. Nonetheless, this word seems to carry few pejorative connotations in its use in *ḥadīth*. It is, however, linked in this passage to *lahw*, a word which is found in legal books with the idea of that [wanton] pleasure, diversion, entertainment, the accompaniment of which makes drinking even legal stimulants reprehensible or forbidden. See Rosenthal, *Gambling*, pp. 19–20.

23. *Risāla fī aḥkām al-qahwa*, ms. Berlin, fol. 11r. See as well Jazīrī, *'Umdat al-ṣafwa*, ms. Paris, fols. 31v–32r; ms. Escurial, fol. 39v.

24. See Joseph Schacht, *An Introduction to Islamic Law* (Oxford: Oxford University Press, 1964), p. 179.

25. Peçevi, *Tārīh*, 1:364.

26. D'Ohsson, *Tableau général*, 4:78.

27. Dufour, *Traitez nouveaux*, p. 38.

28. D'Ohsson, *Tableau général*, 4:81; see also Biddulph, in Purchas, *Hakluytus Posthumus*, 8:266.

29. D'Ohsson, *Tableau général*, 4:81.

30. Osman II, a young, idealistic, and reform-minded sultan was deposed and murdered by mutinous janissaries (although it is not clear where most of the plotting took place), the first clear-cut instance of military regicide (Bayezit II's death after his deposition in 1512 being suspicious but not documented) in Ottoman times.

31. Kâtib Çelebi, *Balance of Truth*, p. 61. Nonetheless, in a survey taken of the town in 1638, mention is made of "repository for grinding coffee, 2," although no coffeehouses are mentioned (see Lewis, *Istanbul*, p. 114).

32. Lane, *Modern Egyptians*, p. 119.

33. *Manqala* is a game of some considerable antiquity (identified also with the game called "Fourteen"), which is played on a board with twelve (or fourteen) hemispherical hollows. Play involves the movement and distribution of counting pieces (twenty-six per player) in the various hemispheres (see Rosenthal, *Gambling*, pp. 43–44; Lane, *Modern Egyptians*, pp. 344–46; Thévenot, *Voyages*, 1:107). Quotation is from Jazīrī, *'Umdat al-ṣafwa*, ed. de Sacy, 1:159.

34. See Rosenthal, *Gambling*, p. 144, where he also documents the existence of specialized gaming houses (*dār al-qimār*) in larger cities.

35. D'Ohsson, *Tableau général*, 4:78, 81.

36. See Rosenthal, *Gambling*, pp. 62–63, where he cites Ettinghausen and Meyer on the existence of playing cards from Mamluk times. Niebuhr (*Travels*, 1:128–29), on the other hand, states flatly that "they knew nothing of our cards." His credentials as a source on social activities are somewhat questionable, since, contradicting all other sources, he says in another place (2:264) that "the Arabians never engage in any game, and sit without entering into conversation with one another." It is probable that if he witnessed such a scene, it was the entrance of his party of Franks which caused the awed suspension of all activity in the first place.

37. Rosenthal, *Gambling*, p. 38.

38. Sandys, in Purchas, *Hakluytus Posthumus*, 8:143.

39. Russell, *Aleppo*, p. 92.

40. Rosenthal, *Gambling*, pp. 87–96.

41. On coffeehouse story-tellers, see Niebuhr, *Travels*, 2:264–66; D'Ohsson, *Tableau général*, 4:81; Kâtib Çelebi, *Balance of Truth*, p. 61; Lane, *Modern Egyptians*, pp. 333, 391, 475; Raymond, *Artisans et commerçants*, p. 519; Russell, *Aleppo*, p. 91. On Persian teahouses, see C. P. Elwell-Sutton, "Čay-Khāna," in *The Encyclopaedia of Islam*, 2d ed., *Supplement*.

42. Russell, *Aleppo*, p. 91.

43. Niebuhr, *Travels*, 1:144.

44. Ibid.

45. Russell, *Aleppo*, p. 91; D'Ohsson, *Tableau général*, 4:81.

46. Jazīrī, *'Umdat al-ṣafwa*, ed. de Sacy, 1:159.

47. Thévenot, *Voyages*, 1:105.

48. See, among others, Dufour, *Traitez nouveaux*, pp. 37–39; Teixeira, *Travels*, p. 62; Lémery, *Treatise on Foods*, p. 317; Lane, *Modern Egyptians*, p. 333.

49. See, for example, Evliyā Efendi's description of Murat IV's gathering of the guilds of Istanbul in 1638 in Lewis, *Istanbul*, pp. 112–13.

50. *Risāla fī aḥkam al-qahwa*, ms. Berlin, fol. 10v.

51. The coffeehouses in London of the Restoration acquired a similar reputation: "These Houses being very many of them professed Bawdy Houses, more expensive than other houses, are become scandalous for a man to be seen in them; which Gentlemen not knowing, do frequently fall into them by chance, and so their Reputation is drawn into question thereby." From an anonymous tract entitled *The Grand Concern of England Explained; in several Proposals Offered to the Consideration of the Parliament. . . . By a Lover of his country,*

a Well-wisher to the Prosperity both of King and Kingdoms (London, 1678), p. 24.

52. Teixeira, *Travels*, p. 62; Sandys, in Purchas, *Hakluytus Posthumus*, 8:146.

53. *Risāla fī aḥkam al-qahwa*, ms. Berlin, fol. 10v.

54. See Rosenthal, *Gambling*, p. 152.

55. John Covel, *Diary* in *Early Travels in the Levant*, ed. J. Theodore Bent, Hakluyt Society, series 1, no. 87 (London, 1893), p. 141.

56. Kâtib Çelebi, *Balance of Truth*, p. 60.

57. Lane, *Modern Egyptians*, p. 333; Russell, *Aleppo*, p. 83. See also Rosenthal, *The Herb*, pp. 19–20, for a discussion of the meanings of the word *banj*–it is apparent here that in this case we are speaking of either hashish or marijuana processed so as to facilitate smoking in the devices available.

58. Rosenthal, *The Herb*, p. 65.

59. Raymond, *Artisans et commerçants*, p. 387; Biddulph, in Purchas, *Hakluytus Posthumus*, 8:266.

60. Rosenthal, *The Herb*, pp. 15–16.

61. Jazīrī, *'Umdat al-ṣafwa*, ms. Paris, fol. 2v; ms. Escurial, fol. 3r. *Fāz 'Abbās*, it seems, is an acronym; it is described in the *Qam' al-wāshīn* as a compound drug, consisting of pepper (*fulful*), opium (*afyūn*), saffron (*za'farān*), pellitory (*'āqirqarḥā*), *banj*, euphorbia (*afarbiyūn*), and spikenard (*sunbul*). See Rosenthal, *The Herb*, p. 33.

62. Jazīrī, *'Umdat al-ṣafwa*, ms. Paris, fols. 30r–30v, ms. Escurial, fol. 39r.

CHAPTER EIGHT

1. Tietze, *Description of Cairo*, p. 37.

2. See Kâtib Çelebi, *Balance of Truth*, pp. 60, 62n.1.

3. See, among others, Abū 'Isā Muḥammad Tirmidhī, *Sunan*, Kitāb al-birr wa-al-ṣila, 10 vols. ([ed. Ḥims, 1965–68], 6:229).

4. Muḥammad ibn Isḥāq al-Washshā', *Kitāb al-Muwashshā*, ed. Rudolph E. Brünnow (Leiden: E. J. Brill, 1886), p. 12.

5. Ibn Ṣaṣra, *A Chronicle of Damascus 1389–1397* [*al-Durra al-muḍī'a fī al-dawla al-ẓāhirīya*], ed. and trans. William M. Brinner, 2 vols. (Berkeley and Los Angeles: University of California Press, 1963), 1:69–72; 2:45–47.

6. Such was the opinion, it should be noted, of one with discernible Sufi leanings. One must wonder, however, to what extent those outside these circles viewed even the connection of coffee with the *dhikr* as laudable, inasmuch as approval of the semi-ecstatic ritual services of many of these orders was not universal, especially among those of a more scholastic orientation.

7. Kâtib Çelebi, *Balance of Truth*, p. 60.

8. Jazīrī, *'Umdat al-ṣafwa*, ed. de Sacy, 1:159.

9. *Risāla fī aḥkam al-qahwa*, ms. Berlin, fol. 11r.

10. In Jazīrī, *'Umdat al-ṣafwa*, ms. Paris, fol. 17v; ms. Escurial, fol. 23r.

11. *Iṣṭifa' al-ṣafwa*, ms. Leiden, fol. 11v.

12. See Muḥammad al-Bukhārī, *Ṣaḥīḥ*, 4 vols., ed. L. Krehl and W. Juynboll (Leiden, 1862–68, 1907–8), 2:75; almost identical stories appear in the other major collections of tradition. On the principle of passing to the right, compare with the coffee ceremony at the Sufi *dhikr* at the Azhar, described above, chapter seven.

13. Ibn Qutayba, *Ashriba*, p. 55.

14. A later association might also have been with the less attractive habits of the rougher and more pagan sort of Mongol or Mamluk, who were known to drink kumiss by circulating the cup. See Maqrīzī, trans., Quatremère (*Histoire des sultans mamlouks*, 2 vols. [Paris, 1837–45]), 2:147n.182.

15. Shams al-Dīn Muḥammad al-Ramlī, *Fatāwā*, in the margins of *al-Fatāwā al-kubrā* of Ibn Ḥajar al-Haythamī, 4 vols. (Cairo, 1357/1938), 4:39–40.

16. Kâtib Çelebi, *Balance of Truth*, p. 61. His complaint is echoed several decades later by an anonymous social critic in Restoration London. Cf., *Grand Concern*, p. 24.

17. William Parry, *A new and large discourse of the Travels of sir Anthony Sherley Knight* (London, 1601), p. 10.

18. Morosini in Albèri, *Relazioni*, series 3, vol. 3, p. 268.

19. Rosenthal, *Gambling*, p. 150.

20. Translated and quoted by Lewis, *Istanbul*, p. 113.

21. Rosenthal, *The Herb*, p. 67.

22. Lane, *Modern Egyptians*, pp. 337–42.

23. S. D. Goitein, *A Mediterranean Society*, 4 vols. (Berkeley and Los Angeles: University of California Press, 1967–), 1:114–15.

BIBLIOGRAPHY

Abū Makhrama al-Ṭayyib ibn 'Abd Allāh. *Tārīkh thaghr 'Adan.* Edited by Oskar Löfgren. 2 vols. Uppsala: Almquist and Wiksells, 1936–50.

Ahsan, M. M. *Social Life under the 'Abbāsids.* London: Longmans, 1979.

al-Anṭākī, Dā'ūd ibn 'Umar. *Tadhkirat ūlī al-albāb wa-al-jāmi' li-al-'ajab al-'ujāb.* 3 vols. [Cairo, 1371/1952].

[Audiger]. *La maison réglée, et l'art de diriger la maison d'un grand Seigneur et autres....* Amsterdam, 1697.

Bacon, Francis. *Historia vitae et mortis.* London, 1824.

———. *Natural History.* London, 1824.

al-Bahūtī, Manṣūr ibn Yūnus. *al-Rawḍ al-murbi' bi-sharḥ Zād al-mustaqni'—Mukhtaṣar al-muqni'.* Cairo, [1380/1960–61].

Beckingham, C. F. "Some Early Travels in Arabia." *Journal of the Royal Asiatic Society* (1949): 155–76.

Bercher, Léon. *La Risâla.* 3rd ed. Algiers, 1949.

Birnbaum, E. "Vice Triumphant: the Spread of Coffee and Tobacco in Turkey." *Durham University Journal* (December 1956): 21–27.

Blegny, Nicolas de. *Le bon usage du thé, du caffé et du chocolat....* Paris, 1687.

Bousquet, G. -H. *Abrégé de la loi musulmane selon le rite de l'imâm Mâlek.* Bibliothèque de la faculté de droit et des sciences économiques d'Alger. Vol. 40. Algiers and Paris, 1962.

———. *Kitâb et-Tanbīh ou, le Livre de l'admonition....* 4 vols. Bibliothèque de la faculté de droit de l'Université d'Alger, vols. 2, 11, 13, 15. Algiers, 1949–52.

Bradley, Richard. *A Short Historical Account of Coffee*. London, 1714.

Brockelmann, Carl. *Geschichte der arabischen Literatur*. 2 vols., 3 supplementary vols. Leiden: E. J. Brill, 1937–49.

Browne, E. G. *Arabian Medicine*. Cambridge: Cambridge University Press, 1921.

al-Bukhārī, Muḥammad. *Ṣaḥīḥ*. Edited by L. Krehl and W. Juynboll. 4 vols. Leiden, 1862–68; 1907–8.

Carne, John. *Syria; the Holy Lands and Asia Minor, Illustrated*. 3 vols. London: Fisher, [1838].

Chamberlayne, John. *The Natural History of Coffee, Thee, Chocolate, Tobacco....* London, 1682.

Cohen, Amnon, and Bernard Lewis. *Population and Revenue in the Towns of Palestine in the Sixteenth Century*. Princeton: Princeton University Press, 1978.

Cotovicus, Joannes [Johannes van Cootwijk]. *Itinerarium hierosolymitanum et syriacum*. Antwerp, 1619.

Covel, John. *Diary*. In *Early Voyages and Travels in the Levant*. Edited by J. Theodore Bent. Hakluyt Society, series 1, no. 87. London, 1893.

D'Ohsson, Mouradgea. *Tableau général de l'empire othoman*. 7 vols. Paris, 1788–1824.

Dozy, Reinhart. *Supplément aux dictionnaires arabes*. 2 vols. Leiden: E. J. Brill, 1881.

Dufour, Philippe Sylvestre. *Traitez nouveaux et curieux du Café, du Thé, et du Chocolate*. Lyon, 1685.

Düzdağ, M. Ertuğrul. *Şeyhülislâm Ebusuud Efendi fetvaları ışığında 16. asır Türk hayatı*. Istanbul, 1972.

Elwell-Sutton, C. P. "Čay-khāna." In *The Encyclopaedia of Islam*, 2d ed.

al-Ghazzī, Najm al-Dīn. *al-Kawākib al-sā'ira bi-a'yan al-mi'a al-'āshira*. Edited by Jibrā'īl Jabbūr. 3 vols. Beirut: American University of Beirut, 1966.

al-Ghazzī, ibn Qāsim. *Fatḥ al-qarīb*. Translation by L. W. C. van den Berg. *La révélation de l'Omniprésent*. Leiden: E. J. Brill, 1894.

Ghūl, Maḥmūd. "Faḍl, Bā." In *The Encyclopaedia of Islam*. 2d ed.

Goitein, S. D. *A Mediterranean Society*. 4 vols. Berkeley and Los Angeles: University of California Press, 1967–.

Goldziher, Ignaz. *Muslim Studies*. Edited by S. M. Stern. Translated by C. R. Barber and S. M. Stern. 2 vols. London: George Allen and Unwin, 1967–71.

The Grand Concern of England Explained; in several Proposals Offered to the Consideration of the Parliament.... By a Lover of his Country, a Well-wisher to the Prosperity both of King and Kingdoms. London, 1678.

Guidi, Ignazio. *L'Arabie antéislamique*. Paris: Paul Geuthner, 1921.

al-Ḥalabī, Ibrāhīm. *Multaqā al-abḥur*. Būlāq, 1265/1848–49.

al-Ḥujāwī, Mūsā ibn Aḥmad. *al-Iqnā' fī fiqh al-Imām Aḥmad ibn Ḥanbal*. 4 vols. Cairo, [1351/1932].

Ibn Ḥajar al-Haythamī, Shihāb al-Dīn Aḥmad. *Tuḥfat al-muḥtāj bi-sharḥ al-Minhāj*. 10 vols. Cairo, [1315/1898].

Ibn al-'Imād, Abū Fatḥ 'Abd al-Ḥayy. *Shadharāt al-dhahab fī akhbār man dhahab*. 8 vols. Cairo, 1350–51/[1931–32]. Reprint. Beirut, 1966.

Ibn al-Jazzār, Nūr al-Dīn Abū al-Ḥasan 'Alī. *Qam' al-wāshīn fī dhamm al-barrāshīn*. Ms. Leiden, cat. de Jong and de Goeje no. 1880 (cod. 814[12] Warn.), fols. 273r–84r.

Ibn Māja. *Sunan*. 2 vols. Cairo, 1952–53.

Ibn Manẓūr. *Lisān al-'arab*. [Beirut], 1955.

Ibn Nujaym. *al-Baḥr al-rā'iq sharḥ Kanz al-daqā'iq*. 8 vols. Cairo, 1311/[1894].

Ibn Qudāma. *Le précis de droit d'Ibn Qudāma* [*'Umda fī aḥkām al-fiqh 'alā madhhab al-Imām Aḥmad ibn Ḥanbal*]. Translated by Henri Laoust. Beirut, 1950.

Ibn Qutayba, Muḥammad ibn 'Abd Allāh ibn Muslim. *al-Ashriba*. Edited by Muḥammad Kurd-'Alī. [Damascus, 1366/1947].

Ibn Ṣaṣra, Muḥammad ibn Muḥammad. *A Chronicle of Damascus 1389–1397* [*al-Durra al-muḍī'a fī al-dawla al-ẓāhirīya*]. Edited and translated by William M. Brinner. 2 vols. Berkeley and Los Angeles: University of California Press, 1963.

al-Isḥāqī, Muḥammad ibn 'Abd al-Mu'ṭī. *Akhbār al-uwal fī man taṣarrafa fī Miṣr min arbāb al-duwal*. Cairo, 1311/1893–94.

Iṣṭifā' al-ṣafwa li-taṣfiyat al-qahwa. Ms. Leiden, cat. de Jong and de Goeje no. 1872 (cod. 1138 Warn).

Jacob, Georg. *Altarabisches Beduinenleben*. 2d ed. Berlin: Mayer and Müller, 1897.

al-Jazīrī, 'Abd al-Qādir ibn Muḥammad al-Anṣārī, al-Ḥanbalī. *'Umdat al-ṣafwa fī ḥill al-qahwa*. Ms. Paris Bibliothèque nationale, arabe no. 4590.

———. *'Umdat al-ṣafwa fī ḥill al-qahwa*. Ms. Escurial, Catalogue Derenbourg no. 1170.

Jorden, Ed. *A Discourse of Naturall Bathes and Minerall Waters*. 3rd ed. London, 1633.

al-Kāsānī, 'Alā' al-Dīn Abū Bakr ibn Mas'ud. *Badā'i' al-ṣanā'i' fī tartīb al-sharā'i'*. 7 vols. Cairo, 1327–28/1909–10.

Kâtib Çelebi [Ḥajjī Khalīfa]. *The Balance of Truth*. Translated by G. L. Lewis. London: George Allen and Unwin, 1957.

Khalīl ibn Isḥāq. *al-Mukhtaṣar*. Paris 1318/1900.

al-Khiraqī, 'Umar ibn al-Ḥusayn. *al-Mukhtaṣar*. [Damascus], 1379/-[1959–60].

La Roque, Jean de. *Voyage de l'Arabie Heureuse*. Amsterdam, 1716.

Lane, Edward William. *An Account of the Manners and Customs of the Modern Egyptians*. 5th ed. Edited by Stanley Poole. London, 1860. Reprint. New York: Dover, 1973.

———. *An Arabic-English Lexicon*. London, 1863–93.

Lapidus, Ira. *Muslim Cities in the Later Middle Ages*. Harvard Middle Eastern Studies no. 11. Cambridge, Mass.: Harvard University Press, 1967.

Leclant, Jean. "Coffee and Cafés in Paris." In *Annales, E.S.C.* 6 (January-March 1951): 1–12. Translated by Patricia M. Ranum in *Food and Drink in History, Selections from the "Annales,"* edited by Robert Forster and Orest Raum, pp. 86–97. Baltimore and London: Johns Hopkins University Press, 1979.

Lémery, Louis. *A Treatise on Foods*. English translation anonymous. London, 1704.

Lewis, Bernard. *Istanbul and the Civilization of the Ottoman Empire*. Norman, Oklahoma: University of Oklahoma Press, 1963.

Löfgren, Oskar. "Bā 'Alawī." In *The Encyclopaedia of Islam*. 2d ed.

al-Maqrīzī. *al-Sulūk li-ma'rifat duwal al-mulūk*. Edited by M. M. Ziyāda. 2 vols. Cairo, 1936–58.

al-Marghīnānī, Burhān al-Dīn 'Alī ibn Abī Bakr. *al-Hidāya*. 4 vols. Cairo, 1326/[1908–9].

Margoliouth, D. S. "Shādhilīya." In *The Encyclopaedia of Islam*.

Melling, Antoine. *Voyage pittoresque de Constantinople et des rives du Bosphore*. Paris, 1819.

Morosini, Gianfrancesco. "Relazione del Bailo Gianfrancesco Morosini (1585)." In *Le Relazioni degli Ambasciatori Veneti al Senato durante il Secolo Decimosesto*. Edited by Eugenio Albèri. Series 3, volume 3, pp. 251–323. Florence, 1855.

Mueller, Wolf. *Bibliographie des Kaffee, des Kakao, der Schokolade, des Tee und deren Surrogate bis zum Jahre 1900*. In Bibliotheca Bibliographica, vol. 20. Vienna: Walter Krieg, 1960.

Mūllā Khusraw. *Durar al-ḥukkām fī sharḥ Ghurar al-aḥkām*. 2 vols. [Istanbul]. 1260/1844.
al-Nawawī. *Minhāj al-ṭālibīn*. Edited and translated by L. W. C. van den Berg. 3 vols. Batavia, 1882–84.
Niebuhr, Carsten. *Travels through Arabia and other Countries in the East*. Translated by Robert Heron. 2 vols. Edinburgh, 1792. Reprint. Beirut: Khayat, n.d.
Pardoe, [Julia]. *The Beauties of the Bosphorus*. London: Virtue, [1839].
Parkinson, John. *Theatrum Botanicum. The Theatre of Plants. Or an herball of a large extent....* London, 1640.
Parry, William. *A new and large discourse of the Travels of sir Anthony Sherley Knight*. London, 1601.
Peçevi, Ibrāhīm. *Tārīh-i Peçevi*. 2 vols. Istanbul, 1281–83/1864–67.
Pococke, Edward. *The Nature of the drink Kauhi or Coffe, and the Berry of which it is made*. Oxford, 1659.
Purchas, Samuel. *Hakluytus Posthumus or Purchas His Pilgrimes*. 20 vols. Glasgow: James MacLehose and Sons, 1905–7.
al-Qayrawānī, ʻAbd Allāh ibn Abī Zayd. *Risāla*. Cairo, [1930].
Quatremère, M. *Histoire des sultans mamlouks*. 2 vols. Paris, 1837–45.
al-Qudūrī, Aḥmad ibn Muḥammad. *Matn al-Qudūrī fī al-fiqh*. [*al-Mukhtaṣar*]. Cairo, 1377/1957.
al-Ramlī, Shams al-Dīn Muḥammad. *Nihāyat al-muḥtāj ilā sharḥ al-Minhāj*. 8 vols. Cairo, 1357/1938.
———. *Fatāwā*. In the margins of *al-Fatāwā al-kubrā* of Ibn Ḥajar al-Haythamī. 4 vols. Cairo, [1357/1938].
Rauwolff, Leonhart. *Aigentliche Beschreibung der Raiss inn die Morgenlaender*. 1593. Reprint, with introduction by Dietmar Henze, Graz, 1971.
Raymond, André. *Artisans et commerçants au Caire au XVIII siècle*. 2 vols. Damascus, 1973.
Risāla fī aḥkām al-qahwa. Ms. Berlin, cat. Ahlwardt no. 5476 (Spr. 1966). Fols. 10b–16b.
Rodinson, Maxime. "Ghidha'." In *The Encyclopaedia of Islam*. 2d ed.
Rosenthal, Franz. *Gambling in Islam*. Leiden: E. J. Brill, 1975.
———. *The Herb*. Leiden: E. J. Brill, 1971.
Rumsey, Walter. *Organon Salutis. An Instrument to cleanse the Stomach, As also divers new Experiments of the virtue of Tobacco and Coffee: How much they conduce to preserve humane health*. London, 1657.
Russell, Alexander. *The Natural History of Aleppo*. London, 1756.
Sacy, Silvestre de. *Chrestomathie arabe*. 2d ed. Paris, 1826.

al-Sakhāwī, Shams al-Dīn Muḥammad ibn ʿAbd al-Raḥmān. *al-Ḍaw' al-lāmiʿ li-ahl al-qarn al-tāsiʿ*. 12 vols. Cairo, 1934–36. Reprint. Beirut, 1966.

al-Sarakhsī, Abū Bakr Muḥammad. *al-Mabsūṭ*. 30 vols. Cairo, 1324–31/1906–12.

Schacht, Joseph. *An Introduction to Islamic Law*. Oxford: Oxford University Press, 1964.

Shaykh-zāde, ʿAbd al-Raḥmān. *Majmaʿ al-anhur fī sharḥ Multaqā al-abḥur*. 2 vols. Istanbul, 1276/[1859].

al-Shīrāzī, Abū Isḥāq Ibrāhīm. *al-Tanbīh fī al-fiqh ʿalā madhhab al-Imām al-Shāfiʿī*. Cairo, 1370/1951.

Teixeira, Pedro. *The Travels of Pedro Teixeira*. Translated and annotated by William F. Sinclair; further annotation and introduction by Donald Ferguson. Hakluyt Society, 2d series, no. 9. London, 1902.

Thévenot, [Jean] de. *Suite du Voyage du Levant*. 3rd ed. 2 vols. Amsterdam, 1727.

———. *Voyages en Europe, Asie et Afrique*. 3rd ed. 2 vols. Amsterdam, 1727.

Tietze, Andreas, ed. and trans. *Muṣṭafā ʿĀlī's Description of Cairo of 1599*. Österreichische Akademie der Wissenschaften philosophisch-historische Klasse Denkschriften, vol. 120. Vienna, 1975.

al-Tirmidhī, Abū ʿIsā Muḥammad. *Sunan*. 10 vols. Ḥims, 1965–68.

Ukers, William. *All about Coffee*. New York: Tea and Coffee Trade Journal Co., 1922.

Ullendorf, E. "Djabart." In *The Encyclopaedia of Islam*. 2d ed.

Ullmann, Manfred. *Die Medizin im Islam*. Leiden and Cologne: E. J. Brill, 1970.

van Arendonk, C. "Ḳahwa." In *The Encyclopaedia of Islam*. 2d ed.

Walsh, Robert. *Constantinople and the Scenery of the Seven Churches of Asia Minor, Illustrated*. London: Fisher, [1838].

al-Washshā', Muḥammad ibn Isḥāq. *Kitāb al-Muwashshā*. Edited by Rudolph E. Brünnow. Leiden: E. J. Brill, 1886.

Watt, W. Montgomery. *Muhammad at Medina*. Oxford: Oxford University Press, 1956.

Wüstenfeld, Ferdinand. *Die Chroniken der Stadt Mekka*. 4 vols. Leipzig, 1857–61. Reprint. Beirut, 1964.

Yule, Henry, and A. C. Burnell. *Hobson-Jobson*. 2d ed. Edited by William Crooke. London: Routledge, [1968].

al-Zaynī al-Ḥusaynī, Muḥammad ibn Maḥmūd ibn Burhān al-Dīn. [*Risāla fī al-qahwa*]. Ms. Princeton, Yahuda coll., catalogue Mach no. 2082.

INDEX

THIS MONOGRAPH WAS COMPOSED USING DONALD KNUTH'S TEX TYPESETTING SYSTEM. IT IS SET IN COMPUTER MODERN TYPEFACES ON AN ALPHATYPE CRS PHOTOTYPESETTER. TECHNICAL WORK HAS BEEN SUPPORTED IN PART BY GRANTS TO THE UNIVERSITY OF WASHINGTON FROM BELL-NORTHERN RESEARCH AND NORTHERN TELECOM, INC.